The Corridors of Time ·III·

PEASANTS & POTTERS

By HAROLD PEAKE and
HERBERT JOHN FLEURE

NEW HAVEN · YALE UNIVERSITY PRESS
LONDON · HUMPHREY MILFORD
OXFORD UNIVERSITY PRESS
1927

OXFORD UNIVERSITY PRESS
LONDON   EDINBURGH   GLASGOW   COPENHAGEN
NEW YORK   TORONTO   MELBOURNE   CAPETOWN
BOMBAY   CALCUTTA   MADRAS   SHANGHAI
HUMPHREY MILFORD
PUBLISHER TO THE
UNIVERSITY

Printed in Great Britain

PREFACE

THE last part of this series, Hunters and Artists, ended with a reference to the great change of climate, which has been one of the most momentous events in the history of mankind. The present volume takes up the story of the crisis in human affairs that followed it. As the deserts spread there was a tendency for people to settle by the margins of the rivers that flowed through the desert areas, and we find a considerable population collecting by the banks of the Tigris and Euphrates and by those of the Nile. Here we find that the people were giving up hunting, as game became scarce, and had taken to agriculture; at the same time we witness the beginnings of the art of stone-grinding and of metallurgy, leading to carpentering and house-building, the invention of pottery and brick-making, and the domestication of animals.

This group of inventions gave men new links with the soil and led to the rise of peasant communities. It also set men to search for new kinds of stone, and enabled them to settle in places where there were no supplies of flint. This, in turn, gave new motives for barter and led to the development of trade. The further consequences of these new opportunities of wider experience will be described in later volumes.

We feel that we should make special acknowledgement of our indebtedness to those who have, within the last few years, so materially increased our knowledge of Ancient Mesopotamia. Suggestions, made years ago, to the effect that South-west Asia was the original home of civilization, and that Egypt in this respect stood second, have now received ample confirmation.

There is still considerable difference of opinion as to the dates that should be attributed to these early phases of civilization, and those that we have adopted will not meet with universal approval. This is inevitable during the present state of this inquiry. The various chronological schemes that have been put forward and our views upon them, together with the reasons that have led us to adopt the dates here suggested, will be given in the next volume of this series, Kings and Priests.

Many thanks are due to the authors, editors, and publishers of the following works and journals for permission to reproduce figures: *Dog Owners' Annual*, 1896 (Dean & Son Ltd.) for fig. 1; *Policing the Plains* by R. G. Macbeth (Hodder & Stoughton Ltd.) for fig. 5; *Explorations in Turkestan*, 2 vols., by R. Pumpelly, W. M. Davis, R. W. Pumpelly, and E. Huntington (Carnegie Institution of Washington) for figs. 8, 10, 52, and 53–5; *The Antiquaries Journal*, vol. i (Oxford University Press) for fig. 22; *The Antiquaries Journal*, vol. iv (Oxford University Press) for figs. 9 (lower) and 36; *Men of the Old Stone Age* by H. F. Osborn (Charles Scribner's Sons) for fig. 11; *Unknown Mongolia* by D. Carruthers (Hutchinson & Co. (Publishers) Ltd.) for fig. 12; *Picturesque North Africa* (Hutchinson & Co. (Publishers) Ltd.) for fig. 56 (right-hand); *Primitive Art in Egypt* by J. Capart (Grevel & Co.) for fig. 13; *Egypt, Descriptive, Historical and Picturesque*, vol. ii, by G. Ebers (Cassell & Co. Ltd.) for fig. 14; *Studies in the Early Pottery of the Near East*, part I, by H. Frankfort (Royal Anthropological Institute) for figs. 15–17 and 38; *Man*, xxv (Royal Anthropological Institute) for fig. 18; *The Journal of the Royal Anthropological Institute*, xli, for fig. 59; *Ancient Egypt*, 1924 (British School of Archaeology in Egypt) for figs. 19 and 20; *Corpus of Prehistoric Pottery* by Professor Sir Flinders Petrie (Bernard Quaritch Ltd.) for figs. 23–7, 31, and 32; *Tools and Weapons* by Professor Sir Flinders Petrie (Bernard Quaritch Ltd.) for fig. 28; *Prehistoric Egypt* by Professor Sir Flinders Petrie (Bernard Quaritch Ltd.) for fig. 29; Chaldaean Genesis by G. Smith (Sampson Low, Marston & Co. Ltd.) for figs. 34 and 40; *Archaeologia*, vol. lxx (Society of Antiquaries) for fig. 35; *Journal of Egyptian Archaeology*, vol. viii (Egypt Exploration Society) for fig. 37; *Die archäischen Ischtartempel in Assur* by W. Andrae (Hinrichs, Leipzig) for fig. 39; *Annual of the British School at Athens* vol. xi for figs. 42, 44, and 49; *Die diluviale Vorzeit Deutschlands* by R. R. Schmidt (E. Schweizerbart, Stuttgart) for fig. 58 (upper left-hand); *Congrès international d'Anthr. et d'Arch. préhist.* 1880 (A. Kundig, Geneva) for fig. 58 (upper right-hand); *Crania Ethnica* by Quatrefages & Hamy (Baillière et fils, Paris) for fig. 58 (lower); *Races of Europe* by W. Z. Ripley (Appleton & Co., New York) for fig. 60; and *A History of Sumer and Akkad* by L. W. King (Chatto & Windus) for fig. 61.

At the same time we wish to express our gratitude to the draughtsmen of the Clarendon Press for their courteous interest and the technical skill which they have devoted to the preparation of the numerous maps and charts.

H. J. E. P.
H. J. F.

September 1927.

CONTENTS

1. The Food Collectors of the North-West . . 7
2. The Fertile Crescent and the Nile . . . 14
3. The Dairy and the Herd 29
4. The Potter's Art 44
5. By the Banks of the Nile 62
6. The Dwellers in Mesopotamia . . . 81
7. The Isles of the Sea 98
8. On the Edge of the Steppes . . . 110
9. Peoples, Nations, and Languages . . . 119
10. Chronological Summary 138

    Index 147

LIST OF ILLUSTRATIONS

1. The Dingo 9
2. Inhabitant of Tierra del Fuego. Photograph by M. Pierre Petit . 12
3. Map of the Fertile Crescent 17
4. Map of Mesopotamia, showing the position of the earliest cities and the sites at which painted pottery has been found . . . 21
5. A log hut in Canada 23
6. A mud hut in the Nile Delta. Photograph kindly lent by Sir Henry Lyons 25
7. A wattled hut in Yugo-Slavia. From a drawing by Bernard Rice. . 27
8. Skulls of *Bos primigenius* and *Bos macroceros* 33
9. Frieze of dairy cattle, from Tell el-'Obeid. In the upper figure a man is seen milking a cow from behind. Upper photograph by Mansell; lower from *The Antiquaries Journal*, IV, by kind permission of the Trustees of the British Museum and the Society of Antiquaries . 35
10. Skull of *Ovis vignei*, from Ladak 36
11. Przewalski's horse 38
12. Mongol horsemen 41
13. Fragment of a slate palette showing sheep and asses. Cairo Museum . 42
14. A water-carrier in Egypt, carrying a goat-skin water-bag . . 45
15. Pottery from Susa I, in the Louvre 49
16. Pottery from Tepeh Musyan 50
17. Pottery from Tell el-'Obeid, in the British Museum . . . 51
18. Badarian arrow-heads. Reproduced, from *Man*, XXV, by kind permission of the Council of the Royal Anthropological Institute and Professor Sir Flinders Petrie 53
19. Slate palettes, flint arrow-heads, and ivory vase from Badari. Reproduced, by the kind permission of Professor Sir Flinders Petrie, from *Ancient Egypt*, 1924 55
20. Ivory figure of Badarian culture. Reproduced, by the kind permission of Professor Sir Flinders Petrie, from *Ancient Egypt*, 1924 . 57
21. Badarian pot. Reproduced, by the kind permission of Professor Sir Flinders Petrie 58
22. Flint implement from Scania, claimed by Montelius to be Solutrean . 59
23. Early wavy-handled pot 64
24. White cross-line ware 67
25. Black incised ware 68
26. Slate palettes 69
27. Decorated pots. The spiral ornament is thought to represent spiral pads of rushes 71

List of Illustrations

28. Early copper daggers 73
29. Native boats of papyrus reeds. From drawings on a painted pot . 74
30. The ivory knife handle from Jebel el Arak, in the Louvre, showing native boats and a foreign ship with a high prow. Photographs by Giraudon 75
31. Decorated pots with boat design 77
32. Wavy-handled pots of native make 79
33. The Weld-Blundell Prism, containing lists of kings. Ashmolean Museum, Oxford 83
34. Back of tablet with account of Flood 85
35. Objects from Abu Sharain, the Ancient Eridu . . . 87
36. Foundation tablet of A-an-ni-pad-da, the second king of the First Dynasty of Ur. Reproduced, by permission of the Society of Antiquaries and the Trustees of the British Museum, from *The Antiquaries Journal*, IV. 88
37. Copper lions from Tell el-'Obeid. Reproduced, by the kind permission of Dr. H. R. Hall, from his article in *The Journal of Egyptian Archaeology*, VIII 89
38. Polychrome ware from the second settlement at Susa . . . 91
39. Pigtailed people of Susa II 93
40. Oannes, the holy fish 97
41. Map of Crete and the neighbouring islands 99
42. Neolithic pottery from Magasá 100
43. Neolithic incised ware. From the Evans Collection in the Ashmolean Museum, Oxford 101
44. Neolithic objects from Magasá 102
45. Stone axes from Knossos. From the Evans Collection in the Ashmolean Museum, Oxford 103
46. Neolithic clay idols, Knossos. From the Evans Collection in the Ashmolean Museum, Oxford 104
47. Predynastic Egyptian bowl, from Knossos. From the Evans Collection in the Ashmolean Museum, Oxford 105
48. Neolithic handles, Knossos. From the Evans Collection in the Ashmolean Museum, Oxford 107
49. Neolithic house at Magasá 108
50. Clay figures of oxen. From the Evans Collection in the Ashmolean Museum, Oxford 109
51. Map of the Caspian region, showing the relation between Mesopotamia and the Turkestan steppe 111
52. Map of the Anau oasis 113
53. Pottery from the first culture of Anau 116
54. Flint implements from Anau I 117
55. Copper objects from Anau I 118

List of Illustrations

56. Hamite and Semite. Right-hand illustration from *Picturesque North Africa* by the kind permission of Lehnert & Landroch, Cairo . 123
57. Map of the Northern Steppe, showing its relations to the Mediterranean, Mesopotamia, and the Indian Ocean 124
58. Broad skulls from Ofnet, Mugem, and Furfooz 125
59. Hittite and Anatolian types 129
60. Western Alpine types 130
61. Ur-Nina and his family 131
62. The Nordic type 135
63. Chart of the early ages in Egypt and Mesopotamia . . . 143

I
The Food Collectors of the North-West

THROUGHOUT the last part of this work we have been following the fortunes of our predecessors in Europe during the gradual retreat of the last glaciation. We have watched them hunting the mammoth and the reindeer on the tundra, the bison and the horse on the cold dry steppe, and the ox and the red deer as the forest advanced. We have traced the various stages of their art and noted the wonderful engravings and paintings on the walls of the caves among which they took refuge during the winter months.

We have seen, too, how, owing to a northward shifting of the storm zone, flanked on the south by a zone of rain-bearing westerly winds that had previously traversed the Mediterranean and the Sahara, the pine forest, followed after an interval by the oak forest, spread from the south-east towards the north-west of Europe until, soon after 5000 B. C., it reached Denmark and South Sweden. The spread of this forest put an end to the hunting of great beasts on open plains, such as had been enjoyed in previous times; and the descendants of the hunters and artists of the Upper Palaeolithic Age settled down by lakes and rivers, or by the sea-shore, and developed the collecting side of their activities. Thus their food consisted largely of shell-fish, nuts, berries, and roots, with the occasional addition of fish and flesh food.

Meanwhile the northward shifting of the westerly winds had reduced the rainfall in the Sahara and was converting that region from a grassy steppe to a sandy waste. Many of the hoofed denizens of that grass-land migrated or perished, while

the men who hunted them scattered in all directions. Some with
'Final Capsian' culture came through Eastern Spain to the
European plain north of the Alps, where they spread the
'Tardenoisian' culture with its 'microlithic' flints. They
for the most part occupied areas with a dry subsoil, such as the
chalk downs, the limestone plateaux, or the patches of sandy
loess, where from lack of moisture the forest was unable to
obtain much of a foothold. These people lived largely on
small game, shot with their bows and arrows, and supplemented
their diet by digging up edible roots with hoes of flint. The
Microlithic culture seems also to have spread to Egypt, where
its sites include the Mokattam Hills, to Palestine, and even to
India and Ceylon.

Then about 4500 B.C. came a slight elevation of the land,
accompanied by a drop in the average temperature causing
a small advance of the Alpine glaciers. This is what we know
as the Gschnitz stage. This drop in the temperature did not
improve the condition of the shore-dwellers, nor, when this
cold period passed and a warmer climate followed, did they
show any material advance in their civilization. They had
settled down into a routine, as had many nature-folk the world
over before European industrialism touched them in the last
century, and it needed some impetus from without to stir them
from the apathetic condition into which they had fallen. Two
items only had they added to their culture, the domestication
of the dog and the discovery of pottery, and we must pause for
a moment to inquire how these otherwise unprogressive people
had obtained these new elements of culture.

The origin of the dog is by no means clear. Studer was of
opinion that in the days of early man a smallish wild animal,
allied to the dog, existed in most parts of Europe and Asia;
this animal he named *Canis poutiatini*. He believed that at

the same time the Dingo was living in Southern Asia; it seems to have persisted quite late in Java. The Turko-Tatar peoples have in their languages a very widespread radical word ' Kuc ', meaning dog, and the position occupied by the dog in their mythology suggests that this animal was owned by them in very ancient times.

FIG. 1. The Dingo.

One of the earliest relics of a domestic dog that has come to light was found in the north Kurgan, or mound, at Anau in Turkestan. These mounds at Anau and the civilizations which they denote will be described more fully in chapter 8. Here we will only say that this dog belonged to a people who had brought the camel and goat to that famous site, and the camel seems first to have been domesticated in Central Asia, or, according to some students, on the Persian plateau. It is difficult to decide whether this dog was derived from the Dingo or from *C. poutiatini*, for in various measurements it is related to both; the latter origin is, however, the more probable. The Anau dog is related to the pariah dog and to the sheep-dog too, and both of these, in all probability, have similar origins.

It is possible that the domestication of this animal may have taken place on two separate occasions, and thus a larger and a smaller form have been tamed; on the other hand divergent breeding may have begun very early. In any case, it would seem that the great dog of ancient Babylonia and Assyria was not derived from the Anau dog, though both may have had the same origin, as may also the dogs of early Greece and Central Europe. Something very like the Anau dog is curiously enough found in Egypt, but it seems likely that this, as well as the long-horned cattle, were brought to the valley of the Nile by an Asiatic people. It appears probable, then, that some at least of the dogs of Ancient Europe were descended from those which were domesticated in Southern or South-Western Asia, though we must bear in mind the possibility of taming the wolf and the jackal, or of hybrids between these animals and early dogs.

It seems very doubtful whether we can derive from West Asia the dogs of the Danish shell-mounds, and the difficulty is still greater with the possibly domestic dog of the Mugem settlement and that from the Azilian deposit at La Tourasse. These belong to so early a period that Asiatic origins seem unlikely, and we are tempted to look to North Africa and perhaps to the movements of the peoples with Final Capsian culture for the earliest dogs of the West.

How our shore-dwelling people of North-West Europe in the early days of the oak forest, with their lowly and unprogressive culture, living in a not too warm but very damp climate, discovered the use of pottery is a much more difficult problem. To those who are convinced that no discovery has been made more than once the answer is clear; it must have been introduced from somewhere else, perhaps from the south-east, for, as we shall see, pottery was known in the Near East at a considerably earlier date. Those, however, who think that similar circumstances will produce similar results have no difficulty either. These food collectors needed vessels in which to store their nuts and berries, and to use, perhaps, for boiling their shell-fish; so to meet this need they found out how to make pots.

We are not convinced that either of these opposing schools of thought has yet proved its case, and we prefer to keep an open mind upon the question. Against the first view is the absence of any evidence of pottery apparently ancestral to that found in the shell-mounds, or, in fact, of any pottery that can be placed at an earlier date, within a thousand miles of the shell-mounds. On the other hand much of the territory to the south-east of Denmark has so far been imperfectly explored, and every year we are receiving fresh evidence of unsuspected early cultures. Against the second view we may urge that the shell-mound pottery shows no sign of its origin. Many wares in their earliest stages show resemblances to gourds, baskets, or leathern vessels, which seem to have given inspiration to the first potters; the shell-mound pots hint at no such prototype.

The rare fragments of pottery from the Danish shell-mounds seem all to have been discovered in the upper layers. We shall, in a later part, see reasons for believing that these mounds continued to accumulate for some time after the arrival of strangers bearing a more advanced culture. We shall then consider whether it is likely that these strangers introduced into Denmark the potter's art.

Save for the dog and the pots, the culture of the peoples of North and West Europe, after the Gschnitz stage, seems absolutely unprogressive, and there are no indications of advance even as late as 3000 B.C. In fact, as we shall see later on, some of these food collectors, farther north in the Baltic, remained in this primitive condition until a much more recent date.

Their methods of life were comparable only to those of the Australian aborigines and the inhabitants of Tierra del Fuego, methods dependent on a hardened routine without production of food and on a low grade of individual initiative. Life on this level is generally characterized by many taboos which hinder progressive change.

FIG. 2. Inhabitant of Tierra del Fuego.

The existence of such a population in North-West Europe in the early days of a climatic régime much like that of our own time suggests some rather important thoughts. It is sometimes said that our climate is such as to evoke the maximum of energy in the human constitution. To this cause has been ascribed the power that the people of North-West Europe have exerted in the world for many centuries past. If, however, the people of this region really remained in a stagnant condition as food collectors for long ages, it is evident that other factors than those of climate enter into the discussion. One undoubted factor is that the care of infants was greatly developed after the change from food collecting to food producing; thus the whole constitution was lifted to a new level of achievement and promise. Another factor is that intercourse and conflict of ideas was necessary in order to liberate initiative from the grip of taboo. In early days in North-West Europe the forest, still unconquered, set great barriers to intercourse and movement, so that the little scattered groups seldom met folks very different from themselves, while their methods of feeding were not of a nature to give a steady supply of energy; for occasional gorging would produce dullness followed by depression, until hunger would ultimately resume its sway. It is generally agreed that regular feeding on grain products, especially wheat, is an important factor of vitality and initiative; and grain plants did not occur wild in North-West Europe.

Leaving for a time these poor unprogressive food collectors of Europe, we must turn our attention eastwards, for, as we shall see, evidence is accumulating to show that the believers in the doctrine of *ex oriente lux* are right, in the main at least, and that the arguments in favour of the opposing doctrine *le mirage oriental* are losing ground, for all the main elements of civilization seem to have been introduced into the West.

BOOKS

MACALISTER, R. A. S. *Text-book of European Archaeology* (1921).
SOLLAS, W. J. *Ancient Hunters* (1924).
OBERMAIER, H. *Fossil Man in Spain* (1924).
CHILDE, V. GORDON. *Dawn of European Civilization* (1925).

2
The Fertile Crescent and the Nile

WE have left for a time the people of North-West Europe, surviving in an impoverished condition after the spread of the forest had put an end to the hunting of great beasts on what had previously been open plains. The northward shifting of the zones of ocean storms and westerly winds had produced an effect, almost as serious, in more southerly latitudes. The Sahara and Arabia became drier, and, though for a while the old hunting life remained possible, game became scarcer and considerable sections of the population were forced to emigrate to the north or south, while some moved eastward from the Sahara to the Nile Valley. In our quadrant of the world the crisis in human life was general, and men naturally turned their attention back to the old habit of collecting food as their hunting became less successful. In certain regions, however, it happened that men were led towards a new idea; it occurred to them to produce food by the cultivation of edible plants. It is important that we should form some estimate of the factors that would move men to act thus, and endeavour to see where such a new mode of life may have started. This problem is as yet one of the most obscure in human history, and any suggestions which we may make should be treated as quite tentative until more evidence is forthcoming.

It is probable that a food collector would clear a space around a plant which was likely to grow so as to give him, or her, food, and this would be likely to happen especially among food collectors in a restricted area such as a small mountain-valley. Myres has also suggested very pertinently, that 'chance seeds and kernels, scattered carelessly, or fruit and nuts, stored squirrel fashion in too damp a nook, may sprout and receive similar care till they are mature enough to repay it'. To Grant Allen is due the suggestion that the idea of cultivation arose from noticing how luxuriant was the growth of plants scattered as an offering to the dead over a newly made grave or placed in the grave as food. The transition from food collecting to food producing, by any of the above or by other analogous stages, would be likely to occur where the ripening of the grain came fairly quickly and thus under conditions of a regular and assured sequence of periods of rain and sunshine. Such a region we must now seek. It should be, moreover, a restricted region, where the inhabitants would not be tempted to wander too widely in search of their food supplies. As yet men were ill-equipped to make clearings in the forest or to drain marsh-lands, so we need not expect to find the first stages of the cultivation of plants in regions of those types. It is well to remember, too, that groups living in a state of isolation are unlikely to have made this great step forward. Men are proverbially creatures of habit, and it is only in some place where men of different traditions have met and mingled that we can expect such a change to have occurred, for the mingling of cultures tends to break down 'taboos' that previously prohibited change.

Taking a survey of the region of light rainfall, we may rule out the Spanish peninsula, for here there does not seem to have been any admixture of peoples of very different cultures; nor were any wild annual plants growing here which could yield a sufficient supply of food. Much the same may be said of North Africa. The Nile Valley played such an enormous part in some of the succeeding stages of history that there has been a disposition in some quarters to claim Egypt as the original home of vegetable food production. In our view Egypt gained its great importance rather later, when further increased drought led cultivators to harness the river-floods. Millet and barley may have occurred wild on or near the Nile, but wheat seems Asiatic, while it also seems that the valley bottom must have been very swampy in those lengths which have since become famous for cultivation by irrigation.

On the northern fringe of the great desert of Arabia is a belt, running from Moab northwards to the foot of the mountains of Eastern Asia Minor and thence south-eastwards along the foot of the Zagros range, which divides Mesopotamia from the Persian plateau. This area, much of it semi-arid now, though it had a moister climate then, is what Breasted has well named the Fertile Crescent. In this region, from very early times, the people of the mountains have come into contact with their neighbours of the steppe and desert. Here, too, are found the wild plants that are supposed, by some observers at least, to be the nearest to wheat and barley. Olivier, indeed, who visited Mesopotamia early in the nineteenth century, said that he found spelt, wheat, and barley growing wild in some ravines not far from Anah on the Euphrates. We cannot, however, build upon this, as his plants may have strayed from cultivated patches in the neighbourhood. Still, if these plants grow wild and untended, the climate must not be very different from that in which they grew before man cultivated them. There seems little doubt that wheat, along with barley, was the earliest plant to be cultivated, but the origin of wheat is much disputed.

In 1906 Aaronsohn found on and around Mt. Hermon in North Palestine a wild form of the emmer, a kind of split wheat; later on he found the same plant east of the Jordan

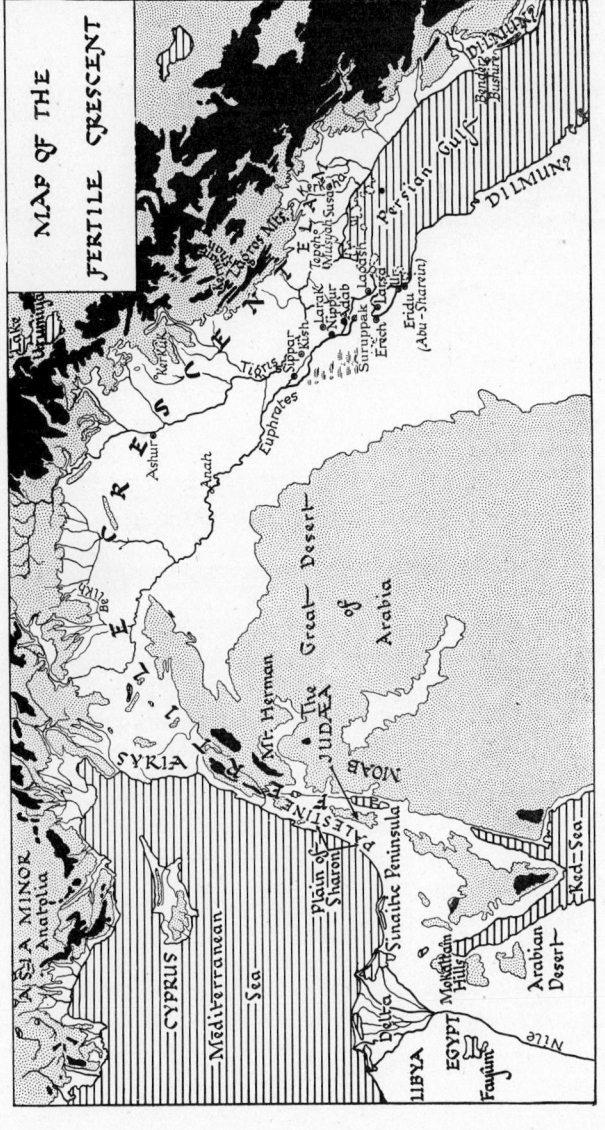

FIG. 3.

in what was once the land of Moab. In 1910 Strauss found a single plant in the Zagros mountains, on the Kermanshah road, almost opposite to Bagdad, but this was no doubt a stray. Körnicke, who examined Aaronsohn's plants, considered them ancestral to cultivated wheat. On the other hand Sir Roland Biffen, who has been working with Aaronsohn's wheat for several years, finds that when crossed with other varieties it produces heads which are so brittle that they are useless for breeding purposes, for the seeds drop from the heads as soon as they ripen. For this reason some authorities believe that it cannot be the ancestor of our wheat. Modern wheats may be divided into three groups :

1. Soft wheats, e. g., *Triticum vulgare*.
2. The emmer group, e. g., *T. dicoccum*.
3. The einkorn, *T. monococcum*.

The origin of the soft wheats is unknown, and Percival has suggested that it is a hybrid between *Triticum dicoccoides*, the emmer found in a wild state, and *Aegilops ovata* or *Ae. cylindrica*. It seems likely that this hybridization occurred in South Russia or Transcaucasia. *T. monococcum* is found wild in South Yugo-Slavia, Bulgaria, and most parts of Greece ; a larger variety is common throughout Anatolia from near Smyrna to Kurdistan and as far south as North Syria. It is also reported from the Crimea. It is a very small grain and is cultivated to-day only in a few poor and backward mountain regions. *T. dicoccoides*, the wild emmer, has been found, as we have seen, from Mt. Hermon to the highlands of Moab ; the claim that its range extended to the Zagros mountains rests on the single specimen found by Strauss.

Since all three types seem to have originated around the eastern highlands of Anatolia, the origin of wheat cultivation is likely to have been at no great distance from this centre.

Barley has been found wild over a more extended region, stretching from Asia Minor to Afghanistan and southwards to Palestine and the foot-hills of the Zagros range. It has been claimed, both by Höck and Vavilov, that wild barley is to be found in North Africa and Abyssinia, but without proof; Schweinfurth, however, records the plant from Tripoli.

On the Anatolian foot-hills there would have been a fair supply of water and an assured succession of seasons, both valuable helps to the beginner in agriculture. The foot-hills cannot have been very densely wooded and so settlement there would have been easy ; the people of the mountains, spreading down towards the plain, would have been far more inclined to make homes than would have their desert neighbours whom they met in this zone.

The earliest dates for such settlements of cultivators are uncertain, but we have indications of very early ones in the plain at Eridu, Badtibira, Larak, Sippar, and Šuruppak (see map, Fig. 4) ;* we know little, however, as yet about the plain. We have seen that about 4500 B. C. there was an elevation of the land and an increase of cold, especially in the mountain regions; this has already been discussed as the Gschnitz stage. The effect of this in the Armenian mountains would be a lowering of the snow-line in the winter, and a consequent increase in the volume of the rivers that drain the area during the periods of melting snow. The Tigris and Euphrates, and especially the latter, which rise in these mountains, would enter the Mesopotamian plain in the spring with much greater force than before or than at the present day; their floods would be of unprecedented size, and we may well believe that many of the riverside settlements were swept away by the hurrying waters and their inhabitants destroyed. Early legends in Mesopotamia contain more than one reference to such a period of floods, and especially to such a destruction of Šuruppak. Another effect of this change was that these floods would bring down great quantities of sediment and spread them over what was, apparently, a somewhat barren subsoil, besides extending the land at the expense of the Persian Gulf. But all the evidence available tends to show that the elements of settled life and food production preceded the floods of the Gschnitz.

Whatever the mode of origin of cultivation, we may safely argue that the use of wild grain for food preceded the beginnings of cultivation, and the indications are that the inhabitants of the Fertile Crescent were aided by some fortunate discovery to substitute food production for the earlier and more precarious scheme of food collection. This gave possibilities of a more settled life with more varied equipment.

The clearing of weeds around a food plant must have been from the beginning a part of the work of cultivation and this has special importance because it at once suggests the use of flint *coups-de-poing* for hoeing. Such use would smooth down the roughnesses of the flint tools and this may have led to the discovery of the art of shaping tools by grinding. The *coup-de-poing* with a broken point would also remain useful if its end were sharpened by grinding into a transverse edge, and so would come into existence the stone axe or stone hoe. It is very important to notice that the ground stone axe, in contrast to the flint *coup-de-poing*, would act as a wedge, and this opened up largely increased possibilities of utilization of wood. It also enabled man to use many kinds of hard rock for his implements. He could thus spread into regions of wooded hills and crystalline rocks, away from the opener plains with their widespread supplies of flint.

The gradual abandonment of the nomadic or semi-nomadic life of the hunter enabled men to have fixed abodes wherein they could keep chattels. We have already seen that the hunters of the Upper Palaeolithic Age had permanent abodes in winter, where they could place in natural cold storage the products of their autumn kills. They developed a vigorous art and possessed a number of chattels, often elaborately decorated. Some of the food collectors of North Europe also seem to have

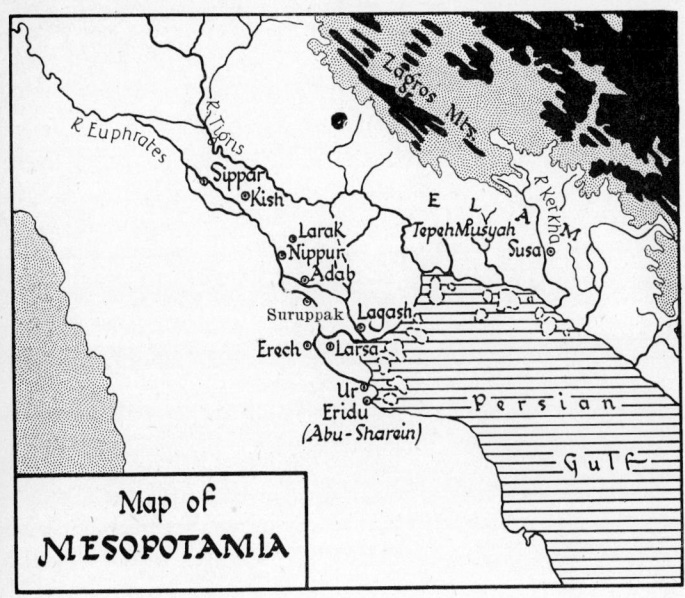

Fig. 4.

had settled habitations, but these were no doubt mean enough, as they had no skill in construction and their time was taken up in gathering their meagre supplies of food. The grain-growers on the other hand required a relatively small part of the year for the cultivation of the ground and the sowing of the crop, and still less later on for harvesting it. At first they had not wholly given up hunting where the land was not too densely populated to make this unprofitable. Later, when game became scarcer, they had probably added domestic animals to their sources of food supply. Whether this was so or not, grain is a more sustaining diet than whelks and limpets, and the grain-growers had more time and more energy to improve the amenities of their surroundings. When the combination of wheat and flesh for food became available the result was an increase of energy and a general strengthening of the constitution.

One of the first needs to be met when man took to a settled existence was protection from the weather for himself and his family, and later, in some cases, for his domestic animals. We have unfortunately no direct evidence of the types of houses first used in the Fertile Crescent or of the materials employed for their construction. We can only conjecture their form and the method of their construction by arguing back from buildings of a later date and comparing them with certain primitive types which survived to later times in other parts of the world. The two chief materials used at first seem to have been wood and mud, though sometimes a combination of both would have been employed.

The inhabitants of the mountains, where the forest had appeared long before, most probably built their houses of wood, and this would have been more easily accomplished in the pine area than in the oak forest. Firs and pines have straight trunks, tapering slowly, and the branches are easily broken off, especially where the tree has fallen and has been dead for some time. We conjecture, therefore, that the first wooden buildings were made of the fallen trunks of coniferous trees. They could have been made in several ways, but we will describe the simplest, because it has survived with little change in the log hut of the north-west of America and it seems to have been

The Fertile Crescent and the Nile

the humble beginning of the type of architecture which culminated in the Greek temple.

Two fallen fir trunks denuded of branches were laid on the ground parallel to one another, the ends, perhaps, resting on flat stones. Two others, somewhat shorter, were laid across these near their ends; then the process was repeated until the four walls reached the height of a man, when a number of

FIG. 5. A log hut.

lighter trunks were laid across the two longer walls and the whole was covered with dry leaves and grass and perhaps finished off with a layer of mud well stamped in. This would provide an adequate shelter but for a few defects, the chief of which were that there was no door and the flat roof would not throw off the rain.

How the door was made in the earliest of such houses it is difficult to conjecture, unless the house was entered through a hole dug in the ground below the bottom log. To-day two vertical cuts are made with a saw through the logs at the end or on the side of the hut, and the sections between these cuts removed. At the very first, in the absence of saws or of as yet effective axes, some other method must have been employed.

In rainy countries the flat roof could be obviated either by omitting the last log on one side and so getting a single slope or more usually by making the end walls one log higher than the side walls and laying a roof-tree across the centre of these, thus forming a flattish gable.

It would soon be discovered that split logs were more suitable for the roof, and the improvement of the wedge which we have already noted made this preparation possible. Such a wedge, tied firmly on to the end of a partially cleft stick, formed a primitive axe, with which considerable advances could be made. Instead of waiting for chance windfalls, the builder could now fell suitable trees for his house; he could now make a door-way, and a window as well if that was required. More important still, grooves or nicks could be cut where the logs intersected at the angles of the building; these would enable each log to lie close to the one below it, thus keeping out the wind. The axe of ground stone once invented led to numberless new inventions, and man had added carpentry to his other arts.

Away from the forest, on the alluvial flats by the riverside, mud was the chief raw material of the builder and we shall see later that a mud wall surrounded the first settlement at Susa, which is probably the earliest village yet known; it seems likely that the houses there were made of the same material. After a time, as it was found inconvenient to carry shapeless masses of mud very far, and as, moreover, such masses were not easy to build with, men took to making rectangular blocks and leaving them to dry in the sun before carrying them to the building; thus were invented the first bricks. These mud houses in Mesopotamia were probably roofed with light

Fig. 6. A mud hut in the Nile Delta.

timbers and thatched with reeds and mud; but in Egypt, where the rainfall is almost nil, they were frequently roofed only with reed mats resting on light poles. By the Nile it was often customary to leave one side of the building quite open.

A third type of house, intermediate between the two already described, grew up by the side of rivers where there was a plentiful supply of willows, poplars, or similar trees. This type of building is known as wattle and daub. A number of light poles was set in the ground about two feet or less apart, with their thin ends uppermost; they were usually set in a ring. Thinner branches were then intertwined round these in horizontal layers as in making a hamper or basket. When the walls had reached a sufficient height, the thin ends of the poles were drawn and tied together, and the wattle-work continued until the domed roof was covered in. The whole outer surface was then smeared with wet clay, which was left to dry in the sun. Sometimes, probably later, such wattled houses were made rectangular in imitation of log huts and roofed somewhat like the latter.

These are only three out of many types which arose in different parts of the Old World in response to various kinds of climate and where different kinds of raw materials were available. We have no remains of the earliest dwellings in the Fertile Crescent, but the evidence at our disposal leads us to believe that they were of one or other of the types described above or variants of these, though sometimes we shall find slabs of stone taking the place of bricks.

When man had erected a house for himself and his family, he would find the need for certain vessels in which to store his food; at any rate his wife would point out to him that such were necessary. Even in his hunting days it seems likely that he had used some of the skins of the beasts he had slain to make

Fig. 7. A wattled hut in Yugo-Slavia.
From a drawing by Bernard Rice.

receptacles for carrying water, perhaps even for cups, though in some lands horns were used for the latter purpose. Leather vessels no doubt continued in use after he had given up his nomadic habits, but as hunting gave way more and more to agriculture skins became scarcer and other types of vessels were needed. Those who lived in wattled huts soon saw that they could make smaller objects by the same method, and so baskets were made; it is just possible that the order was reversed and it was basket-makers who first thought of making wattled huts. Allied to this, for the technique is nearly the same, is the making of reed and grass mats, an art that was developed in Egypt at a very early date. From this to the development of weaving was a very short step. Besides leather and basketry other things were used as vessels, especially dried gourds, which grow wild in Asia Minor and the Fertile Crescent, but the most important of all was pottery.

It has been suggested that the idea of pottery arose from the practice of smearing baskets with clay to make them hold water and to withstand the effects of fire. This may be so, for both the forms and especially the decoration of some pots suggest a basket prototype. On the other hand this resemblance may be due to the adoption of the potter's art, introduced from without, by a people who had hitherto used only baskets as vessels. This explanation would apply, too, to pots resembling gourds or leather vessels. It seems more likely that the idea of pottery came from the wattled hut, as probably did that of basketry, but from one that had been accidentally burned. The baked clay from the ruins would be a vivid object-lesson in the properties of this material, and might well lead the way to the making of pots and bricks.

Two other discoveries or inventions followed rapidly after a fixed home had been achieved. It was discovered that certain stones when sufficiently heated became liquid enough to be run into moulds, and it was found out that, by scratching certain pictures on slabs of clay or on stone, messages could be sent to a distance. But how the arts of metallurgy and writing arose must be left to a later chapter, though we may point out here that their beginnings are nearly if not quite as old as agriculture and a settled home.

BOOKS

NEWBERRY, P. E. 'Egypt as a Field for Anthropological Research.' The Presidential Address to the Anthropological Section of the British Association (1923).
SMITH, G. ELLIOT. *The Ancient Egyptians* (London, 1911).
STAPF, O. 'The History of Wheats.' Suppl. to *Journ. of British Agriculture*, xvii (1910).
PERCIVAL, J. *The Wheat Plant* (London, 1921).

3
The Dairy and the Herd

EARLIER anthropologists were wont to recognize three successive stages in the evolution of human civilization, the hunting, the pastoral, and the agricultural, and it was assumed that all societies that had reached the third stage must of necessity have passed through the other two. We have now abandoned that view. We must admit that a hunting stage preceded the other two forms; we may admit that an agricultural stage is higher, as measured in material comforts, than the pastoral; but we must admit, too, that some peoples have passed from a hunting or collecting stage direct to the agricultural. This will be clear when in the next chapter we examine the evidence from the first settlement at Susa, the earliest agricultural village yet discovered, and later on when we discuss the village at Anau. At both these places we find evidence of the cultivation of grain and of the entire absence at first of domestic animals. We have not yet succeeded in probing sufficiently far into the earliest phases of either of these stages, the agricultural and the pastoral, to determine which has the priority; the inference is, however, that both began almost at the same time, but in response to different environments, and that both had passed their initial stages by 5000 B.C.

It is well known that before the introduction of the horse into North America by the Spaniards the redskins hunted the bison on foot. They drove large herds of these animals for hundreds of miles across the prairies, making pitfalls, driving herds over precipices and slaying any that wearied and fell behind the herd. The men of the Upper Palaeolithic Age must have hunted in some such way, especially the Solutreans, who came into Europe after the bison and the horse, and who, for the most part, moved off eastwards on the spread in Western Europe of the pine forest.

There are long stretches of sandy loess in Galicia just north of the Carpathians extending intermittently to South Russia and the Roumanian plain; another similar mass in the north of Hungary connects with this by easy passes. These loess areas would have been grassy steppes and would have continued eastwards across Russian Turkestan to the foot of the Hindu Kush. Similar steppes of a colder nature run northward along the Ob and merge in the tundra of Siberia.

Over this great grassy region, we believe, the descendants of Solutrean men long continued to hunt the hoofed denizens of the steppe, and here, if we may trust to the distribution of microlithic flints, they were joined by some of the more adventurous of the Final Capsian invaders, who had been driven by drought from the Sahara, or by people who had been in contact with them. Just north of the steppes, especially in Russia, is a broad belt of park-land, where groves of trees mingle with grassy glades, the woods getting thicker and thicker as we proceed north, until they pass imperceptibly into dense oak forest. This park-land was specially the home of herds of wild cattle, which roamed the steppes in the late spring but retired later in the year to the park-lands again. It seems probable that the calves were born rather in the park-lands than in the open steppe, for they are unable to run fast during the first few weeks of life. In a state of nature they would be born in the early spring, almost as soon as the snow had melted, and a month later, just when the steppe grass would be at its best, they and their mothers would be ready to wander in the open.

If we think of the descendants of Solutrean man hunting wild cattle on the Eurasiatic steppes as the redskins hunted the bison on the American prairies, we can imagine that sometimes they were able to surround the herd and control its movements. This may not be considered exactly as domestication, but it would have been a long step in that direction. The herd and the human group under whose control it had come would wander together seeking fresh pastures, passing at the appropriate seasons from steppe to park-land and back again, while the human group would take toll of its animal companions as the need for provisions required. Eventually, as the two groups gradually became more familiar with one another, relations would become less strained and ultimately a woman with an infant would be able to coax a cow with a new-born calf to share its milk between the offspring of both. In other lands, where sheep or goats were the prevalent wild beasts, similar methods would be employed; except that sheep, at any rate, are more docile than cattle, and in time can be led, while cattle need always to be driven.

Cattle, as we have seen, are not only denizens of the steppe but also of the park-land, and, if sufficient open glades are to be found, they may penetrate far into the forest country. When the oak forest spread over Europe it did not wholly exterminate them, for the urus, a long-horned species, not only lived in the west during Magdalenian times, but was killed in Neolithic days and survived wild in some parts of Europe as late as the time of the Roman Empire.

The urus, called by Bojanus *Bos primigenius* and by Rütimeyer *Bos palaeotaurus*, ranged all over Europe and Asia, excepting the peninsulas of Arabia, Hindustan, and Malaya, during most of the Pleistocene period, though it appears not to have occurred wild in Africa; it seems to have survived over most of this tract into much later times. By degrees the Asiatic members of the species became slightly differentiated from their European neighbours, especially in the form of the horns. This Asiatic variety was found wild in North India by Falconer and Cautley, who named it *Bos namadicus*; a similar form was named by Duerst *Bos macroceros*, though he later admitted its identity with *B. namadicus*.

The cattle, found in a domesticated state in the early settlements of Mesopotamia and Turkestan, seem to belong to this species, which is also found in Egypt during the early dynasties. The conditions accompanying domestication resulted in a considerable diminution in the size of the animal, and also in the length of its horns, so much so that Duerst is of opinion that the small short-horned animal, found in the Swiss Lake-dwellings and named by Rütimeyer *Bos brachyceros*, is but a much diminished form of the same species.

Cattle must have strayed many a time up the rich open meadow lands, often to be found in mountain valleys in the midst of dense forest, and such sheltered nooks with rich

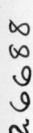

FIG. 8. Skulls of *Bos primigenius* and *Bos macroceros*.

feeding would often be sought by cows as the time of calving drew nigh. Here was an opportunity for the less adventurous dweller in the mountain valleys to make the cow a prisoner with her calf, either by lassoing her with a rope of twisted grasses or by driving her into a rough corral made of fallen pine trunks. The cow could with coaxing be persuaded to give some of her milk to her jailer; by constant feeding with rich meadow grass she would become much tamer; then after a time she could be trusted out on the hill-side in the summer, because she would be certain to return to her prison and an ample supply of food when the snow made it difficult for her to obtain it for herself.

After several generations of such captivity, coupled with gentle treatment, a mild breed of cows would be obtained, which would mix with wild consorts on the hills in the summertime and return home when the snow fell. Later on, as the daily milking became a necessity, they would be trained to roam by day and return to the settlement at eve. As we have seen, the result of this domestication was reduction in size, and further variations must have been produced by cross-breeding, intentional or otherwise, and eventually by selective breeding.

Such events may well have happened more than once in the fertile valleys of the wooded mountain region between the steppe land and the Fertile Crescent. No fierce hunting people could have achieved such a result. It must have been a people of mild and gentle manners, such as are often found among the hill-folk of the central mountain range, who could so have tamed the cow. Where this was effected we know not, but we have evidence, as we shall see later, of the existence of a dairy cult in Mesopotamia, at Ur of the Chaldees, not very long after 4000 B. C., and as the cows there were very tame, the initial experiment must have been made centuries before.

Many species of wild sheep have been recognized by zoologists, but Duerst is of opinion that the *Ovis orientalis* of Gmelin, the *Ovis arkal* of Brandt, and the *Ovis vignei arkal* of Lydekker are all varieties of the same species; he believes, too, that the *Ovis aries palustris*, the turbary or marsh sheep of the Swiss Lake-dwellings described by Rütimeyer, is but a domesticated descendant of the same species.

Sheep of this species ranged wild over most of the mountain

FIG. 9. Frieze of dairy cattle, from Tell el-'Obeid.

country of Asia, at any rate from the Punjab to Armenia, while a variety of this species roamed the steppes to the north. In Turkestan the people of Anau at an early date had domesticated the variety that ran wild in the Kopet Dagh mountains, and it seems probable that all domesticated sheep have been derived by selective breeding and crossing from the types found in this part of Asia. The Barbary sheep, the only species found wild in North Africa, has never been domesticated.

The goat is found wild over most parts of Central, Eastern,

and Southern Asia, though it does not occur on plains or at low altitudes. It is thought that it also ran wild in Crete and in many of the islands in the Mediterranean. Whether it roamed wild also in the highlands of Europe is uncertain, and there is no evidence that it was wild in North Africa.

FIG. 10. Skull of *Ovis vignei*, from Ladak.

So far we have been considering the domestication of animals used for food, whether as flesh food or as supplying milk; another use was made of wild animals at an early stage by converting them into beasts of burden. In the Old World the chief beasts employed for this purpose are the ass, the camel, and the horse; the ox has been used to draw the plough and the wagon, but this was probably a somewhat later development. The Yak serves as a beast of burden in Tibet, and in that country sheep are used to carry loads of borax to the plains below.

The wild ass, *Asinus taeniopus*, is a native of the steppe lands of North-East Africa, and may perhaps have spread over South-West Asia. It is thought that this beast may have been domesticated at an early date by the predynastic peoples of the Nile Valley; it was certainly tamed by the Libyans on the desert to the west of that valley, from whom it reached the valley-dwellers not long after 4000 B.C. The same beast was used by the Sumerians in Mesopotamia, but it is not clear whether they had acquired it at a very early date. On the evidence available at present it looks as though the ass was first tamed on the Libyan desert, but we have to admit great blanks in our knowledge concerning the desert of Arabia and the lands surrounding it. It is possible that it was tamed independently in both continents.

The two-humped camel seems to be a native of Central Asia and is at home in the dry steppes and deserts of that continent; it has been found wild near Lop Nor. It was known early to the inhabitants of Arabia, and it has been thought that they had bred these animals from a very early date, as a figure of a camel has been found in a First Dynasty tomb in Egypt. It has been stated that it was used as a beast of burden by the Egyptians during the Middle Kingdom, but this view rests on no certain evidence. It is, however, essentially a desert dweller and does not maintain itself in the Nile Valley. Duerst thinks that the one-humped camel is a native of North Africa. The first appearance of this beast in Mesopotamia is about 1000 B.C.

The horse is, as we have seen, a native of the dry, open steppe, and seems to have developed in Asia, where Przewalski's horse still runs wild. In late Aurignacian times it spread, as we have seen, all over Northern Europe, but with the extension of the forest it retreated again to the east. Like the cattle, however, some few remained behind, picking up an existence in the open glades of the forest and around the marshes of North Germany. Here they survived for long, and many were tamed during the later phases of the Bronze Age. Some kept their liberty still later, and it has been stated that there were wild horses in the Vosges mountains as late as the reign of Francis I of France.

All the available evidence indicates that the horse was first

FIG. 11. Przewalski's horse.

tamed in some part of the Asiatic steppe. The more lowland portion of this steppe runs from Galicia intermittently to South Russia, and thence continuously across Russian Turkestan with a narrowed eastward extension of varying relief reaching right away to the Sea of Okhotsk. This steppe belt is bounded on the north mostly by pine forest, but belts of steppe or meadow near the North Asiatic rivers give a more or less forest-free link between steppe and tundra. The west part of this steppe was inhabited from Magdalenian times onwards by descendants of Solutrean man, reinforced later by the more adventurous of the Final Capsian invaders. The highland steppe desert of the Tarim and Mongolia was probably long uninhabitable owing to glaciation, but it became the home of broad-headed types commonly known as Mongols. The inhabitants of both steppes have long been famous horsemen, but we do not know which tamed the horse.

As we have seen, our first positive evidence of domesticated cattle dates from about or not long after 4000 B.C. and of the domesticated ass from about the same time. Of the horse we have no positive evidence much before 2000 B.C., but then we know little of the life on the steppes during the earlier centuries. The general inference is that all the animals domesticated in the Old World were tamed before 5000 B.C. Different animals may have been tamed at different places under different circumstances, in fact to meet different needs, and the same animals may have been tamed in more than one place. This would at first lead us to suppose that the idea of taming animals arose independently in different regions. This need not, however, have been so.

We have already seen reason to suspect that before their dispersal from the Sahara and adjoining deserts the Final Capsian folk had tamed the dog, a useful aid to hunting. Some of these folk ultimately reached the Eurasiatic steppe, where we believe herds of cattle first to have been got under control. These steppe-dwellers may well have tamed the horse too, or their Mongol neighbours may have learned from them the advantages of domesticating animals and anticipated them in respect of the horse. The earliest dairymen in the mountain valleys may well have dwelt in the mountains fringing the steppes and received the idea of domesticating the cow from watching the half-tamed herds of the nomads on the plain below.

It is likely that at an early date there was intercourse between the Eurasiatic steppes and the arid regions of Persia and Arabia, and that the knowledge of domestication passed that way, as it did to the early Sumerians of Ur. Or these people, being but an eastern extension of the early Sahara-Arabia men, may have had the dog, and like their northern kinsmen may have thought of taming sheep and goats, and in Libya the ass too, though our first evidence of this is not much earlier than 3400 B.C. We know too little at present to do more than point out possibilities, but it is clear that on the present evidence both solutions are possible: that based on the principle of diffusion from a single centre and that which attributes several origins to the various arts.

Thus two types of culture arose almost simultaneously in regions not very far apart, the pastoral and the agricultural. One might perhaps better describe them as three, for the pasturage of flocks and herds in the open steppes, whether the beasts were cattle or sheep and goats, was a very different occupation from keeping a few milch kine and their calves, tame and to some extent in confinement. The first group wanted beef or mutton, and milk was only of secondary importance; the other depended mainly on milk and cheese, and for flesh used only that of the superfluous bull-calves.

Though these three cultures arose, founded respectively on the dairy in the mountains, grain in the foot-hills and the valley bottoms, and herds on the steppes, there was at first little interchange of ideas. The nomad herdsman, always on the move, would not find it convenient to grow grain, and came to look with disdain upon the manual toil it involved. The settled husbandman had no time or space to keep large flocks or herds, which might at any moment trespass into his fields and demolish his crops. The people of the desert and steppe and those of the foot-hills and valleys lived different lives in different environments, and mutually despised one another.

FIG. 12. Mongol horsemen.

The former feared the nomad as much as they objected to his flocks and herds, while the dwellers on the steppe had no words bad enough for the people living in the cities of the plain. Thus arose the enmity that has always existed between those who gain their living from the fruits of the soil and those whose

FIG. 13. Fragment of a slate palette. Cairo Museum.

wealth consists of flocks and herds. Such a feud is the basis of the story of Cain and Abel, told by Abel's kinsmen and from Abel's point of view, and of similar legends to be found in the early traditions of other peoples.

Between the grain-grower and the dairyman relations were different. Both had adopted a settled mode of life, both were of a peaceful temperament. A small and docile dairy-herd was a useful adjunct to the arable farm and could be bedded on the superfluous straw. The patient tiller of the soil, who with foresight stored till next season some of the products of his crops, soon learned to cut the rank grasses by the river-side, to dry them and to store them for his cattle's winter food. The dairyman, too, found grain of service, for hunting was difficult in the mountain woods. With the hoe, with which he had aforetime dug up roots to help to fill his meagre larder, he cleared small patches on the hill-sides for his grain, and, when the slope was so steep that the rain washed away the soil, he built up low walls of rough boulders to keep it up; this served the double purpose of retaining the soil and freeing the little fields from large stones. Thus arose terrace cultivation. Soon the inhabitants of both mountain valley and alluvial flat had both grain and dairy cattle, more grain in the lower ground and more milk and cheese above. In the highest mountain reaches the goat was substituted for the cow, but milk and cheese were still the main products.

Thus the dwellers in the valleys and in the plains came into close contact and had much in common, and both feared the nomad of the steppe. One thing, however, they borrowed from him—his beasts of burden. We find in predynastic days in Egypt the dwellers in the Delta receiving asses as well as other beasts from the Libyans of the African desert, and it seems likely that the dwellers in Mesopotamia were similarly drawing asses from the tribes on their borders. Even the folk in the mountain valleys found in time that this patient animal can carry in the firewood and thus earn his share of the grass and hay.

4
The Potter's Art

IN the last chapter we have seen that emmer, a kind of wheat, and barley as well, grew wild in the Fertile Crescent. We have suggested, therefore, that it was within this area that the cultivation of these grains was first practised. On the other hand, both of these grains were used at a very early date in Egypt, and many writers have claimed for the dwellers by the Nile the distinction of being the first agriculturists. Before we can decide these rival claims we must examine the origin and early development of another craft, the potter's art.

The cultivation of grain involves a considerable amount of fairly continuous work, though in its earlier stages this work was neither as arduous nor as continuous as in modern civilized communities. The cultivators would therefore be encouraged to settle in permanent abodes in close proximity to their crops. This is, of course, not an absolute necessity. The nomad Bedouin of the Libyan desert sow crops of barley in the desert just south of Alexandria and then depart on their wanderings, returning home to reap the crop if it has survived the early summer drought. The Shawiya, who live in stone villages in the Aures mountains in Southern Algeria, occupy a treeless region where fuel is entirely absent. Every autumn, when the crops have been sown, the majority migrate with their families and their flocks to the province of Constantine, a well-wooded region, where they camp and burn a supply of charcoal for the year. In March, their labours ended, the caravan sets off for home, where they arrive in ample time to harvest their crops.

FIG. 14. A water-carrier in Egypt.

In spite of these exceptions, and many others might be cited, there is a tendency for cultivators of grain to settle permanently beside their fields. It is even probable that the first cultivators in the Fertile Crescent had already somewhat abandoned the roving life of the hunter, owing to the drying of the deserts, and had settled down, like their contemporaries in Europe, as food collectors, before they discovered the advantages of cultivating grain; it seems highly probable that these collectors had long been in the habit of using wild grain for food before it occurred to one of them to clear the ground about the wild plants and then to sow the first patch of grain.

Even in his nomadic days man must sometimes have needed vessels in which to carry water, but, among hunters, these would have been made of skins, like the goatskin vessels of the Eastern water-carriers. As collecting and provision for the future became more important, other vessels will have been needed in which to store his nuts and berries; these were often made of basket-work, or sometimes, where the necessary raw material was available, of dried gourds. How, when, and where the first vessels were made of baked clay is still uncertain, and it is our purpose to pursue the inquiry farther in this chapter. We shall find that some of the earliest known seem to have been made in imitation of leathern vessels, though later we shall meet with others the ornament of which suggests baskets or gourds.

At the foot of the Zagros mountains, near the River Kerkha, stood the city of Susa, the winter capital of the ancient Persian kings (see map, Fig. 3). The site of this city was explored between 1891 and 1907 by a French expedition under the direction of M. Jacques de Morgan, and here they found remains of a number of superimposed settlements. We are concerned only with the lowest and earliest, the remains of which were found 25 metres below the top of the mound.

The Potter's Art

It would seem that at an early date there were a number of little hillocks bordering the Kerkha River, and on one of these, rising about five metres above the plain, some nomads from the higher country behind made a settlement. They built a little town or village surrounded by a wall of beaten earth, and outside this lay the cemetery in which they buried their dead. The bodies were laid to rest in many different ways, but each had the same type of equipment; vases, from three to five in number, were placed at the head, and the men had copper axes of simple form, wrapped up in linen cloths, while the women had round copper mirrors and little cosmetic pots. These people used flint implements; it is thought that they practised agriculture, but they seem to have had no domesticated animals, except the dog and perhaps the horse. Their pots were well made of fine clay, were very thin, and were decorated in black on a pale buff ground with a somewhat standardized ornament. Great quantities of this ware are to be seen in the Louvre, and it has been discussed recently with much acumen by Mr. H. Frankfort.

Frankfort has shown convincingly that this pottery is formed on a leathern model, though he admits that in one or two examples the decoration is suggestive of basketry. The vases from the graves are so thin and so porous that they could never have held liquids, and he has suggested that they were dummies put into the graves to represent the leathern pots which were in everyday use. Frankfort considers the style of decoration very young and vigorous, and believes that it has no long history behind it, although in several points the technique is far from primitive. For instance, the pots were made on a tournette, a slow wheel turned by hand, and the black paint used for decoration was ferruginous earth mixed with some alkaline substance as a flux. As can be seen from some of the scenes depicted on the vases, the people of this settlement lived largely by hunting, which they did with the aid of dogs. It has been supposed that they had tamed the horse, but this rests upon one doubtful representation of that animal on a bowl; it seems more likely that if they knew the horse, they knew it, like the men of Solutré, as a beast to hunt. That they were acquainted with agriculture we infer from the discovery of corn-grinding stones in the mound, which are thought to belong to the bottom layer. The exact stratigraphic position of these grinding stones is uncertain, but we shall find evidence later which will lead us to think that some, at any rate, belong to this civilization.

After a time we find certain foreign elements in this civilization, and to these Frankfort attributes a northern origin. Some of the graves contain turquoise, which is not found in this region; in others there is obsidian, which is thought to have come from Alagheuz in Armenia. There are also some stamp-seals and a few vases of red pottery, both of which Frankfort would bring from Asia Minor or North Syria, from the area, that is to say, which was later dominated by the Hittites. The point is far from clear as yet, but we shall find many reasons, as we proceed with our inquiry, for suspecting the early presence of a civilization in North Syria, probably at no great distance from Aleppo, from which have radiated elements of culture to enrich its neighbours. Above the layer containing these intrusive elements comes a sterile layer one or two metres in thickness, from which it has been conjectured that the people whom we have been discussing were forced to abandon their homes, perhaps owing to drought, perhaps to floods.

About 150 kilometres from this place, a little north of west, about 1,000 feet above the sea and more than 500 feet above the level of Susa, lie a series of hillocks, one of which is known

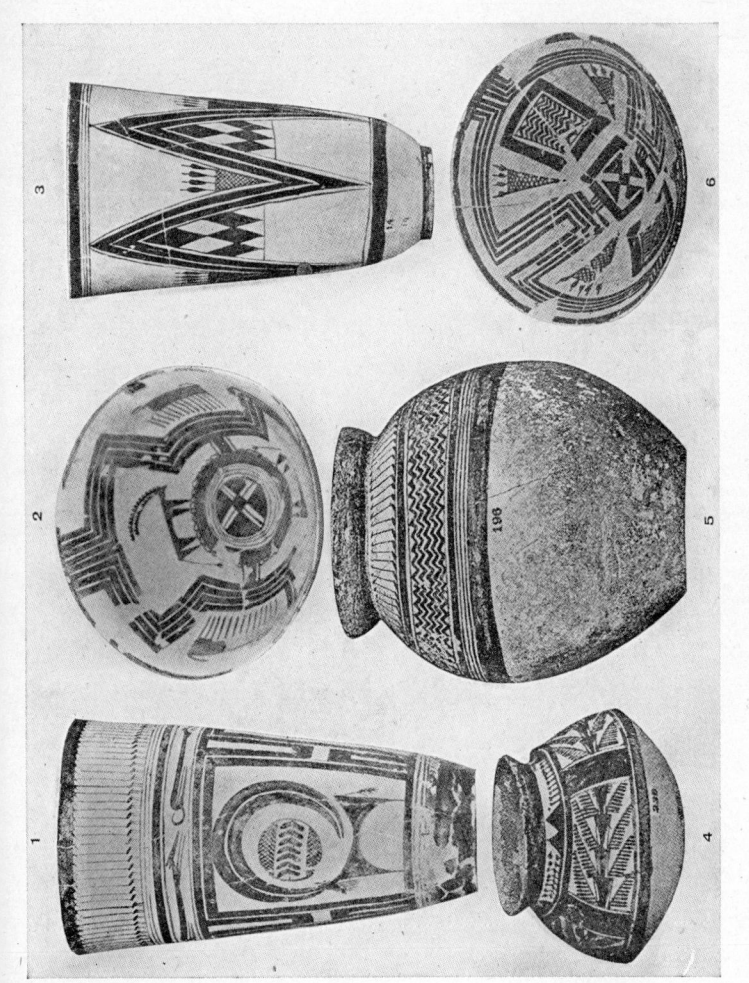

FIG. 15. Pottery from Susa I, in the Louvre.

as Tepeh Musyan. These were explored in 1903 by MM. Gautier and Lampre, and here were found a number of pottery fabrics, resembling in many ways those from the lower layer at Susa. Here were found thin vases, like those from Susa, but apparently somewhat later in date, and a thicker ware, of the same type, representing, as Frankfort thinks, the household pottery of the same date. But below this, and apparently belonging to a people ignorant of metal, were some fragments

FIG. 16. Pottery from Tepeh Musyan.

of hand-made pots, of reddish clay, in some instances rough and decorated with incised or relief ornament, in others burnished and with geometric designs in red paint. Pottery not unlike this has been found at Bismya, the ancient Adab, and a single vessel of this type comes from near Lake Urumiya in North-West Persia.

This last type of pottery presents an interesting problem, which cannot be solved until more material is forthcoming, but it suggests the possibility that earlier pottery fabrics than those found at Susa may turn up to the north or north-west of that site. The later pottery seems to hint that after the site of Susa had been abandoned, the Tepeh Musyan site, well away from a river and more than 500 feet higher, remained occupied

The Potter's Art

by the same or an allied people. The fact that the higher site remained longer occupied suggests that the abandonment of the earlier site was due to floods, perhaps to some of those spring floods which, as we have seen, would have occurred during the Gschnitz period.

Further, fine painted pottery, resembling more closely that of Musyan than that of Susa, has been found by Mr. Campbell

FIG. 17. Pottery from Tell el-'Obeid, in the British Museum.

Thompson and Dr. Hall at Abu Sharain, the ancient Eridu (see map, Fig. 3), and by Dr. Hall and Mr. Woolley at Tell el-'Obeid near Ur; other wares of similar type have been found by M. Pézard at Bender Bushire. These three series of pottery are all so similar that we must consider them to be contemporary, and it is conjectured that they are probably rather later than the wares of Tepeh Musyan. The graves containing this ware at Abu Sharain were considerably lower than the earliest Sumerian graves, and the same appears to be true at Tell el-

'Obeid. Among the early Sumerian objects occurred similar drab pottery, not painted as a rule, though there was 'an occasional recurrence of apparently degenerate painting'. With the Abu Sharain pottery were found flint hoes, ground stone axes, flint flakes, arrow-points, corn-grinders and querns, sickles and spindle-whorls, but apparently no metal. It is clear that these people, though they depended to some extent on the chase, were cultivators of grain, and this makes it the more probable that the early inhabitants of Susa were also grain-growers.

When M. de Morgan first described his discoveries at Susa, he was struck by the enormous accumulation of debris, and basing his calculations on more recent deposits in the Nile Valley, he suggested that the occupation of the site dated back to about 18000 B.C.; and this date was accepted by Montelius, as has been mentioned by Myres in the *Cambridge Ancient History*. But dates based upon the accumulation of debris on occupied sites may be very misleading, and few archaeologists felt disposed to accept these calculations seriously; before his death de Morgan suggested 5000 to 4500 B.C. as a date for the foundation of the settlement.

If Frankfort is right, and we are inclined to agree with him, the settlement at Susa came to an end before that of Tepeh Musyan; Susa, and perhaps Tepeh Musyan, had ended before Abu Sharain and Tell el-'Obeid began. The two latter, especially the last, preceded by a long time the Sumerian culture of the first dynasty of Ur. The beginning of this, as we shall see later, is variously dated between 4000 and 3000 B.C.; we must, therefore, place the stone age graves at Tell el-'Obeid far back in the fifth millennium. If we are right in believing that Susa was abandoned owing to floods—and the fact that the culture lasted later at the higher site at Tepeh

Musyan lends colour to this—we may well believe that it was abandoned during the Gschnitz stage about 4500 B.C., and we may place the lower Mesopotamian sites slightly later, when the period of floods was past. Then de Morgan's date of 5000 B.C. will not be unreasonable for the foundation of the first settlement at Susa, and we should feel disposed to place it rather before than after that date.

We must now return to the problems of the Nile Valley. Through the arid region running from the Atlantic to the Persian Gulf and beyond, a deep channel, formed mainly by a complex series of geological faults in Pleistocene times, carried waters from the rainy regions in the south down to the Mediterranean Sea. This valley passed through many vicissitudes during the Pleistocene epoch, and after the last glaciation, or as some would say before it, the valley bed became filled with an alluvial deposit.

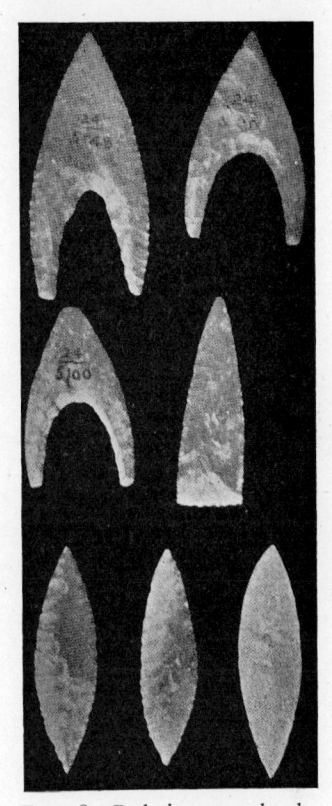

Fig. 18. Badarian arrow-heads.

This deposit is being added to by the annual overflow of the Nile, and attempts have been made to date the age of the alluvium by comparing its depth with the present annual deposit. But it has been our contention throughout that the climate of Europe and the surrounding regions has varied from time to time owing to the shifting of the westerly winds from the Atlantic. This would mean that the amount of matter carried in suspension by the river has been subject to great variations. Moreover, we have been arguing for considerable changes of level between sea and land farther north, for numerous oscillations in the coast-line, so that, if our contention is correct and the oscillations affected North Africa, not only has the rate of deposit in the valley bottom varied from time to time, but the valley has also been subject to erosion, when part of the former deposit has been worn away to be filled up again later. These factors make it impossible for us to accept dates based upon the idea of a uniform rate of deposition.

The dry climate of Egypt and the nature of its soil are such that objects buried in the ground are better preserved there than elsewhere. The reverence paid to the bodies of the departed since quite early days has brought into existence a vast series of cemeteries, well furnished with evidence of contemporary culture, extending continuously over a long period of time. Lastly, for more than a century extensive excavations have been carried on, some scientifically, others merely for loot, so that the mass of evidence available for the study of the civilizations of the Egyptians more than equals that obtained from all other regions put together. It is not surprising, therefore, that many writers claim Egypt as the home of most elements of civilization, while one school of thought believes that in this valley are to be sought the source and origin of them all.

With these views we are by no means in agreement, and in the matter of the cultivation of grain we are inclined to give the palm to Asia, for no evidence has been forthcoming that emmer has been found wild in Egypt either in modern or in

The Potter's Art

earlier times, though barley may have grown wild in the north. The subject is, however, full of complications, and we must leave its fuller discussion to a later chapter.

We have seen that some groups of hunters with microlithic

FIG. 19. Slate palettes, flint arrow-heads, and ivory vase from Badari.

or Final Capsian culture had been occupying the Mokattam Hills; evidence of the presence of these people has also been found on the limestone ridge which fringes the Delta on the north, and which was then, we believe, raised higher above the sea than at present. These people seem mostly to have avoided the valley, which was very marshy at that time, and to have hunted on the high ground on either side, which would not have been so dry as at present. A little later a new culture appeared in this region.

Early in 1924 Brunton, working for the British School of Archaeology in Egypt, discovered in the Badari region near Qau, above Assiut, this new culture, which had been called Badarian. This was at first believed to be contemporary with the earlier predynastic graves, and may well, as we shall see, be merely an earlier phase of the culture that they illustrate; recently Sir Flinders Petrie has claimed for it a greater antiquity. These remains were lying below layers in which were found remains of what are said to belong to the earliest phase of the predynastic period. There were two layers of these Badarian remains, separated from one another by about six inches of sterile soil.

During the winter of 1924-5 Miss Caton-Thompson, working for the same school, found in the desert north of the Fayûm further deposits, which are considered by Petrie to belong to the same culture, though we believe them to be much later in date.

No full description of either of these sites has been published as we write, and we have to describe them from a few short papers which have appeared, some in the daily press, from the specimens which have been exhibited at University College, London, and from information kindly supplied by Sir Flinders Petrie and Miss Caton-Thompson. From these sources we gather that the chief distinguishing features of the Badarian culture are small bowls of fine thin ware with a polished black surface, a globular vase of buff pottery with four small handles, flint arrow-heads deeply notched at the base, human figurines in ivory, which are thought to represent two human types, and a number of flint implements of oval shape and finished with pressure flaking, which bear some resemblance to the finer works

FIG. 20. Ivory figure of Badarian culture.

of the Solutrean industry. These, however, are not all, for Brunton writes that in one untouched grave of this culture at Badari he found 'two or three beads, made of narrow copper ribbon', while in another grave 'was a stout copper pin or borer'.

Soon after its discovery Sir Flinders Petrie claimed a Solutrean origin for this industry, and, since the discoveries north

FIG. 21. Badarian pot.

of the Fayûm, he has claimed for them a Solutrean date. He has applied to the deposits of the Fayûm a method of dating based on the annual rate of deposition of the alluvium, a method that we believe for reasons already given to be very unreliable, and from calculations based on this method he has argued for an early date, on one occasion 13000 B.C. and on another from 12000 to 10000 B.C.

As we do not see our way to approving the method we cannot accept this dating as evidence of Solutrean workmanship, and it remains to discuss whether it may show ultimately Solutrean influence. Now flint and obsidian implements with a pressure-flaking technique are found in many parts of the world, including America, and some anthropologists have claimed a remote Solutrean ancestry for all of these. Towards the close of the stone age in Denmark we find flint knives or daggers of a very Solutrean appearance, and it is by no means easy in all cases to distinguish these from true Solutrean weapons; in fact not long before his death Montelius claimed one such, found in Southern Sweden, which had been somewhat water-worn, as a true relic of Solutrean times, though this view has not received the support of any of his archaeological compatriots. These finely flaked daggers, which are found in tombs known as passage graves and date from about 2000 B.C., were very probably introduced by invaders from the south-east, who entered Jutland some centuries earlier and brought thither the stone battle-axe with a shaft-hole. Similar implements, with the pressure-flaking technique,

FIG. 22. Flint implement from Scania, claimed by Montelius to be Solutrean.

have been found at Susa in the first period, and others have been picked up on the surface in Palestine and the Sinaitic peninsula. Spindle-shaped implements of flint with a similar finish have been found in many places on the northern edge of the Sahara, and are believed to date from late neolithic times, which there may be as late as 1000 B.C. or even later.

A few ground celts, made of black rock, have been found at Badari, apparently in association with Badarian remains. These occur nowhere else in the Nile Valley, but are not uncommon in Asia Minor and Mesopotamia. Myres has put forward the very useful suggestion that these were first made out of trapezoid pebbles, ground as wedges with which to split wood, somewhere in or near Asia Minor, and in a former chapter we have elaborated this suggestion. Those discovered with the fine painted ware at Tell el-'Obeid are of the usual Asia Minor form, but of softer stone and with flattened sides; it must be noted that some of the Badarian celts also have their sides ground to a flat surface.

While we do not feel disposed for the reasons given to admit the Solutrean date of the Badarian culture, we cannot altogether dismiss the idea that some of its features may be ultimately of Solutrean origin. We have seen in the last part that as the pine forest spread in Northern Europe the hoofed animals of the steppe disappeared, apparently to Asia from whence they had come, and that following them most of the Solutrean hunters departed too. Certain regions in South Russia long remained grassy steppes—some parts would be so to-day were not corn grown there in abundance—and beyond the Volga to the slopes of the Hindu Kush great grassy steppe-lands extend throughout Russian Turkestan. To this steppe-land we believe Solutrean man retired, and here we believe he survived until fairly recent times. In a later part we shall come across evidence of a people, apparently nomadic in their habits, who bear some resemblance to the men of the Solutrean epoch. Some of these we shall trace in later times passing across Europe to the Baltic a few centuries before the appearance of the Solutrean-like daggers in the passage graves of Denmark. It is possible, therefore, that some thousands of years earlier some of these dwellers on the steppes passed southwards, picking up trapezoid celts in Asia Minor and the art of pot-making somewhere else; that they gave to the ancestors of the Susa folk their technique of pressure-flaking, and passed on to Egypt as the authors of the Badarian culture. Some such movement seems at the moment possible, but much more evidence is necessary before we can claim it as even probable.

One result, not perhaps quite conclusive, appears from this discussion, namely that the Badarian pottery is probably some of the earliest yet known, though that contained in the lower layers at Tepeh Musyan, and perhaps at Susa as well, may be of the same period, and that perhaps it dates from a little before 5000 B. C. On the meagre evidence at present at our disposal we should be inclined to suggest that the first pottery was made, from leathern models, somewhere not far from the sources of the Tigris and Euphrates, or between that region and North Syria. This suggestion is hardly more than a guess, and fresh archaeological research may any day show that it is untenable, or may on the other hand, perhaps, confirm it.

BOOKS

FRANKFORT, H. *Studies in Early Pottery of the Near East*, i (London, 1924).
Cambridge Ancient History, vol. i (Cambridge, 1923).
MORGAN, J. DE. *Prehistoric Man* (London, 1924).

5

By the Banks of the Nile

THE richest and most continuous civilization yet studied is that which grew up by the banks of the Nile. We have seen that about 6500 B. C. the rainfall in the Sahara and Arabia diminished, and many of the inhabitants of these regions moved to better watered lands; and so we find microlithic flint implements, very similar in form but known under such names as Final Capsian and Tardenoisian, spread over large areas in Europe, Asia, and Africa. These appear, too, in the valley of the Nile; as we have seen, they have been found on the Mokattam Hills and on the northern fringe of the Delta. Their distribution throughout the valley has not yet received much attention, still less their stratigraphical position, so from such evidence we can form no idea of their date; it is only from the occurrence of like flints elsewhere that we can presume that in the Nile Valley, too, they date from 6500 to 6000 B. C., and may have remained in use till a much later time. Of the culture of the men who made and used them we know nothing; we may infer that they gained their living mainly, probably entirely, from the chase, and we have seen reason for believing that they had tamed the dog.

In a former chapter we have described the newly discovered Badarian culture. We have found reason for suspecting that the people responsible for its introduction to the Nile Valley were a nomadic folk, who had passed across South-West Asia, picking up elements of culture on their way, arriving at their final destination about 5000 B. C. In the Nile Valley they seem to have had fairly settled abodes, though there is as yet no evidence that they cultivated grain or owned domesticated animals; we must, therefore, imagine for the present that they lived partly by hunting and partly by collecting such natural products as the banks of the Nile would supply. Their finely worked flint spear-heads and arrow-points and their pottery formed on a leathern model suggest that they had not long abandoned a nomadic hunting state, though they had ground celts and a little copper.

It is, however, with the graves known as predynastic that the continuous history of Egyptian civilization begins, and it is to these that we must devote this chapter. As all students of Egyptian history are aware, early writers have left us lists of kings of that country, divided into dynasties, beginning with Menes, the founder of the first dynasty, who was the first to weld the whole country into one kingdom. The period beginning with Menes and ending with the conquest of the country by Alexander the Great, during which Egypt was ruled successively by thirty dynasties, is called the dynastic period; the period immediately preceding this is known as the predynastic. Various dates have been adopted for the accession of Menes, and these we shall discuss at length in the next part; here we shall only state that in this work we are following that adopted by Professor Breasted, which is about 3400 B. C. This then we shall take as the closing date of the predynastic period, and it remains for us next to discuss that of the earliest predynastic graves yet discovered.

We have, it is true, no direct evidence from which we can deduce the length of the predynastic period, but, thanks to Petrie, we have a method of subdividing it and so of placing in relative chronological position each grave or settlement. This method, known as 'sequence dating', was invented by Petrie when reporting on the remains from Diospolis Parva. He noticed that on certain pots a wavy ridge of clay appeared where a handle should be and that in other pots this ridge degenerated until nothing was left but a line scratched upon the pot; other forms of degeneration accompanied the disappearance of the ridge. This enabled Petrie to place the pots in chronological order, and by noticing what other objects

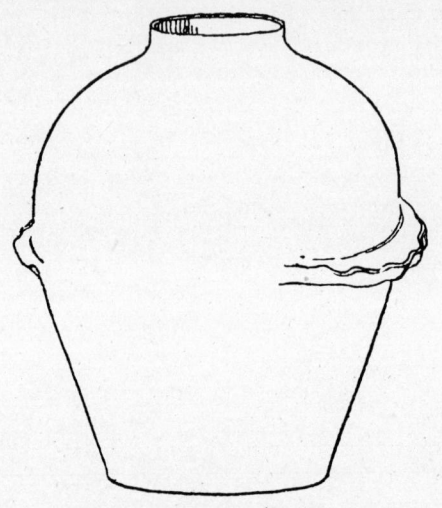

FIG. 23. Early wavy-handled pot.

appeared in association with them he was able to give sequence dates to the remainder. The period covered by this method of sequence dating was divided into about 70 parts, each with its appropriate number from 30 to 100. Nos. 1 to 29 were left blank, so that room might be left for any future discoveries of earlier date, while No. 79 is contemporary with the early years of the reign of Menes, which began, according to the system we are adopting, about 3400 B. C.

Petrie has suggested that the predynastic period, covered by the sequence dates 30 to 78, lasted for about 2,000 years; this we are inclined to consider a rather generous estimate. Some writers have maintained that it is impossible to make an estimate which is not pure guess-work, as there is no certainty that the periods represented by the sequence dates are even approximately of the same duration. We feel, however, that, though the length of each sequence period may vary, the average for any ten is not likely to be very different from that of any other ten, except that the earlier periods would be somewhat longer than the later. We have, therefore, endeavoured to make an estimate on these lines.

The predynastic period is usually divided into three sections: Early, 30–39; Middle, 40–59; Late, 60–78; while 79–100 seem to cover roughly the two first dynasties. Now the average length of the last 21 numbers is about 20 years, and we are suggesting that, if we allow an average of 25, 30, and 35 respectively for those classed as Late, Middle, and Early, we shall have a scheme that is not far from the truth. This will make the duration of the predynastic period 1,425 years, somewhat less than Petrie's estimate.

Before, however, we begin our description of this civilization we must see what the country was like, that we may appreciate the background of the drama. For this we shall follow the account given by Newberry, who is not only an experienced Egyptologist but a botanist as well. He pictures the Nile Valley at this time as having a moister climate with a richer vegetation, and the bed of the valley, which has now for a long time past been intensely cultivated, as a series of undrained swamps full of papyrus and other reeds. The crocodile and hippopotamus were common in the lower reaches of the river, as indeed they were until comparatively recent times, while on either side of the marshes and on into the deserts roamed vast herds of antelopes of many kinds, Barbary sheep, and wild asses.

Such was Egypt when the Badarians entered the valley, nor had it changed when the predynastic culture first arose. In such surroundings we may picture the first settlements that were made at the edges of the marshes above Cairo, and, though no direct evidence has been found, we are justified in believing that similar settlements were made at the same time, or perhaps even earlier, by the sides of the Delta. The graves of s. D. 30, which according to our calculations would have begun about 4825 B. C., were very poorly furnished, each containing only one pot of finely burnt red ware with a black top. In s. D. 31, however, we find with black-top pots another ware, called white cross-line ware; these are pots evidently made in imitation of basket-work, for the ornament consists of rectilinear designs in chalky white paint on a reddish wash.

Frankfort has questioned the correctness of placing the graves of s. D. 30 in a period by themselves, and would treat them as poor graves of a later date. He is inclined to believe that the two kinds of pottery arose simultaneously. To this we cannot agree. The black-top ware seems to us to be derived from the Badarian, though there may have been intermediate stages, examples of which have not yet been found; Badarian in its turn is copied from leather models. The white cross-line ware is clearly copied from originals in basketry, and though, as Frankfort insists, it is young in style, the examples that we have are clearly not the earliest attempts.

It seems to us unreasonable to suppose that two such distinct styles, one decorated and the other plain, each with its own distinctive form, arose simultaneously in the same region. The black-top ware is more widely distributed and continues later, besides showing signs of derivation from the earlier fabric of

Badari. We agree, therefore, with Petrie that it is earlier and native, while the white cross-line ware has been introduced from elsewhere. While, therefore, we believe that there are graves with simple black-top pots which can be placed with confidence in S. D. 30, we think it possible that some of the graves figured under this heading may be, as Frankfort suggests, poor graves of later date.

The white cross-line pottery then represents a foreign

FIG. 24. White cross-line ware.

element that entered the Lower Nile Valley at the beginning of S. D. 31, which we should place about 4790 B. C. Petrie suggests that this was brought in by Libyan settlers, but, since the ornament clearly is derived from baskets made of rushes or grasses, we think it less likely that it came from the desert than from some other region along the marshes. The entire absence of this ware from Nubian graves proves that it did not come down the river; it may well have come up-stream. We are in complete ignorance of the culture of the Delta at this time, though we can hardly believe that the margins, at any rate, of its marshes were uninhabited. From this region we should be inclined to bring the makers of this new ware; if from the western margin, they were no doubt of Libyan affinities; not so, however, if they came from the eastern side. The white crossline ware lasted but a short time, during s. D. 31–34, after which it is rarely if ever found. It does not die out gradually, for

FIG. 25. Black incised ware.

more types were in use during s. D. 34 than in any other of the preceding periods; its sudden disappearance must mean the departure of the people responsible for it at the end of s. D. 34, about 4675 B. C.

Another type of ware, also derived from basketry, makes its appearance about the same time; this is a black ware with incised geometric designs. This black incised ware is first met with in s. D. 33 and occurs, though never plentifully, almost throughout the predynastic periods. Although, like the white cross-line ware, its decoration is based on basket models, there is clearly no connexion between the two wares, which must have grown up independently, though in a somewhat similar environment. It seems tempting to believe that these two

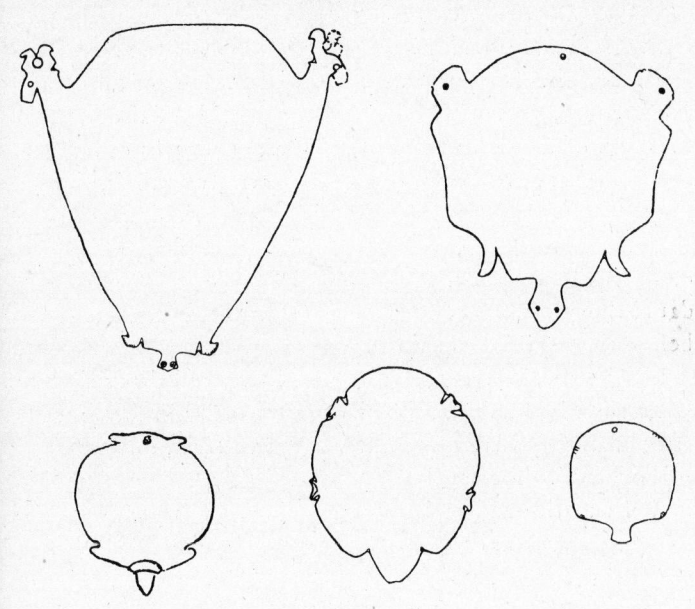

FIG. 26. Slate palettes.

basket wares developed on either side of the Delta marshes, and since we shall presently find reasons for suspecting that the black incised ware may have come from the western bank, we may think of the white cross-line ware as developing on the eastern side of the Delta.

It is difficult to determine with precision the culture of the people of the Early Predynastic Period, for many items are claimed for the predynastic period as a whole by writers who do not state clearly to which period or sequence date must be referred the evidence on which their statement depends. These early folk lived mainly, if not entirely, by hunting, and remains of gazelles and of other kinds of antelopes have been found among the rubbish-heaps that they have left behind, but there is no reason for believing that they possessed domesticated animals. They probably collected the seed of the millet, *Panicum colonum*, which grew wild by the side of the marshes, for seeds of this have been found in the stomachs of some of them; but we have no evidence that they cultivated this, though they may have grown barley. They were undoubtedly fishermen, and seem to have invented a kind of canoe made of bundles of reeds tied together. Their houses were made of wattle and daub, though bricks of Nile mud, dried in the sun, were used before the beginning of the dynastic period.

Like the Badari folk they used flint knives and slate palettes; at first the latter were rhombic or rectangular in form; soon afterwards they were made in the shape of birds, tortoises, and hippopotami. These palettes were used for grinding pigments, both haematite and malachite; the latter was used to paint the eyes, a custom known to have been in use in early dynastic times. Malachite, which is an ore of copper, is said to have been found in the mountains in the Sinaitic peninsula, to reach which must have involved a long journey for these early Nile dwellers; this, however, is uncertain, for the word translated 'malachite' might mean 'turquoise'. Copper silicate has, however, been found in the Wadi Samara. Since it can be shown that green stains and other evidence of the use of malachite date back to Badarian times, we must admit not only that these early people discovered malachite or acquired it from their neighbours, but that in later times there was a constant trade in this commodity with the dwellers in Upper Egypt. By such channels, too, must have come those rare copper objects which we meet with in the Badarian and Early Predynastic periods. We need not suppose that at this early date the Nile dwellers had learned the art of working in metal. In this way, too, may have arrived the idea of cultivating grain.

It was at the beginning of s. d. 38, or about 4545 b. c., that we find new forms of pottery appearing in Middle Egypt. One of these forms, characteristic of the Middle Predynastic Period and to be described later, is clearly copied from stone models, and stone bowls and vases seem first to have been made in the Arabian desert, which lies between the Nile and the Red Sea; here stone is still used for many purposes for which other materials are employed elsewhere. According to Frankfort people from this region seem to have been drifting in by the Wadi Hammamat between s. d. 38 and 42, and it was their arrival that so changed the culture of the Nile dwellers as to enable us to speak of a distinct Middle Predynastic Period; Newberry, however, would bring others up the Nile from the western corner of the Delta. They were not, however, the only new-comers. At the very beginning of the Middle Predynastic Period, s. d. 40 or about 4475 b. c., we notice the appearance of another new ware of plain pottery with wavy handles, which comes ultimately, as Frankfort has shown, from North Syria. Frankfort thinks that they arrived in Egypt full

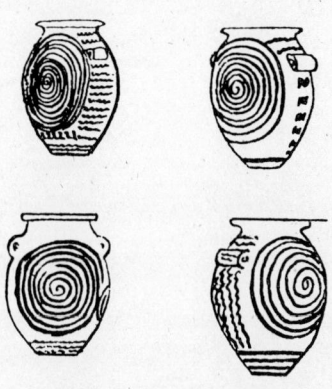

Fig. 27. Decorated pots.

of oil as an article of commerce, and this may perhaps be true for Middle Egypt. Newberry, however, has shown that about this time a people from Palestine, but ultimately from North Syria, settled in the Delta, bringing with them the knowledge of grain, the worship of Isis and Osiris, and many other important cultural features. He doubts whether olive oil formed the chief contents of the wavy-handled pots, and suggests spices, resins, and such-like substances. As the wavy-handled pots begin to reach Middle Egypt by S. D. 40, it seems likely that the new settlers in the Delta had arrived there somewhat earlier, at or even before S. D. 38. We may think of these newcomers as first introducing the knowledge of metal-working into the Nile Valley.

We must, then, consider the intruders as men from North Syria, perhaps broad-headed, who were tillers of the soil and who introduced into Africa the cultivation of emmer and perhaps barley as well as cattle. To judge by analogies in Asia they had brought with them the germs of a calendar, based solely on the phases of the moon; that is to say they measured time not by years but by months. In Egypt, however, owing to the regular summer rise of the Nile, it became necessary to have a solar year, and at first this seems to have been one of 12 months of 30 days. Greater accuracy was soon achieved, and a year of 365 days was inaugurated in the year 4241 B. C. How this date has been arrived at will be explained in a later part.

It seems probable that these invaders brought in the knowledge of spinning and weaving and the cultivation of flax. These arts had been known earlier in Asia, as we have seen from the things found in the early graves at Susa. It seems likely, too, that in their original home they had been accustomed to some form of picture-writing, and devised a scheme of their own after their arrival, for, as Newberry has shown, many of the signs that were later employed in their hieroglyphic writing were taken from plants that thrived only in the Delta.

It would appear strange at first sight that two such movements into the Nile Valley should occur at almost the same moment. The fact that this happened makes us suspect one of those changes in level or climate which we have found causing simultaneous movements elsewhere. We have seen that in the Baltic region a slight elevation took place about 4500 B.C. and lasted for a few centuries; this we have considered as corresponding to the Gschnitz stage in the Alps. The terraces on the African shore of the Mediterranean, described by Depéret and Lamothe, show us that such movements have been felt in North Africa, and it seems likely that a rise of 25 or 30 feet took place in the Delta. This change would have come about gradually, and its greatest effects would have been noticeable between 4600 and 4400 B.C. The land would have been raised well above sea-level, which would have caused the mouths of the Nile to deepen their channels; thus the great mass of the Delta would have been changed from an impassable morass to a well-drained alluvial plain. Such a plain would have been tempting to cultivators of grain, who had, we may well believe, already passed south from North Syria to the fertile Plain of Sharon in Palestine. We have based our estimates of the duration of the predynastic periods on the assumption that

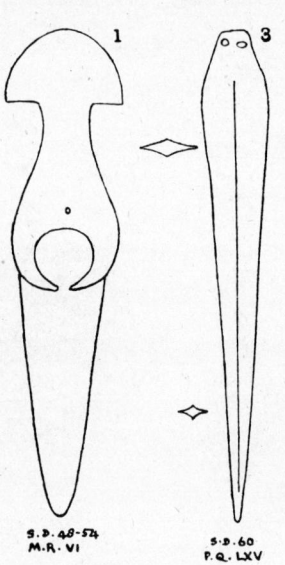

FIG. 28. Early copper daggers.

this change of level in the Delta was a sufficient reason to account for the arrival of a new people. Their arrival was, we believe, the cause which first brought the most important elements of culture into Egypt, whose inhabitants had already learned how to make pots and who knew of the existence of copper from the much earlier Badarian hunters; they had, apparently, also invented a river boat or raft, constructed from bundles of papyrus reeds, and perhaps cultivated barley.

FIG. 29. Native boats of papyrus reeds.

The causes that led the inhabitants of the Arabian Desert to descend the Wadi Hammamat into the Nile Valley near Keneh north of Thebes are more obscure, but any rise of land would make the river cut its channel deeper and thus increase the area of dry river plain, and the rise affecting the Delta may have been felt even as far south as this. Such enlarged dry shelves just above the river would tempt the tribes living in the desert behind to settle nearer the water. If they came from the Delta, they may have been driven southwards by the people from Syria.

We now come to the Middle Predynastic Period in Upper Egypt, opening with s. d. 40, which we have dated about 4475 b. c.

Frankfort is inclined to see in the arrival of the new-comers on the Upper Nile merely a case of peaceful penetration, but the great change in the pottery and the abundance of pots of

FIG. 30. The ivory knife handle from Jebel el Arak, in the Louvre.

the new style of decorated vases betoken an invasion in force. Though these new-comers belonged to the same racial type, we imagine that they made themselves masters of the river-side villages. The Syrian culture probably arrived peacefully along trade channels, but the settlements in the Delta were not effected without a struggle, as can be seen by the illustration on the knife from Jebel el Arak, which dates from about this time. Here we have clearly depicted a severe fight between two peoples of different types, one of which has landed from a boat of foreign build, which shows us that some, at least, of the invaders arrived by sea.

The most noticeable new element in the Middle Predynastic Period is the painted pottery introduced by the intruders from the Western Delta. This ware has been compared to that of the early Susans; but, as Frankfort has shown, it differs from it in the colour of the clay and paint, in the form of the pots and the designs of the decoration. One form is derived from stone pots, which were introduced into the valley about this time, while the decoration at first consisted mainly of spirals, which seem to indicate frames of rush-work with which the stone pots had been covered for protection. Later we find drawings of river scenes and especially of boats. It would seem that some of the intruders, coming fresh from a dry and stony land into an alluvial valley, began to make pots in imitation of the stone vases that they had used before, decorating these pots with designs taken from the rush-work cases in which the stone vases had been slung. The ovoid pots, on which boats are pictured, seem to have been introduced from the Western Delta.

The wavy-handled pots of Syrian origin came in slowly, brought evidently by traders from Palestine or the Delta. About S. D. 46, 4295 B. C. according to our calculation, they became more common, showing that a regular trade had been established. About S. D. 58, or 3935 B. C. by our calculation, the numbers increased considerably; this seems to betoken a regular trade by sea. In S. D. 62, about 3825 B. C., early in the Late Predynastic Period, the importation of these foreign types abruptly ceased.

Slate palettes, usually in the form of fish or birds, still continued in use; ivory combs, for scratching the head, were plentiful and bone harpoons were common. Flint knives became more finely flaked, while copper objects, rare at the close of the previous period, became more abundant, especially

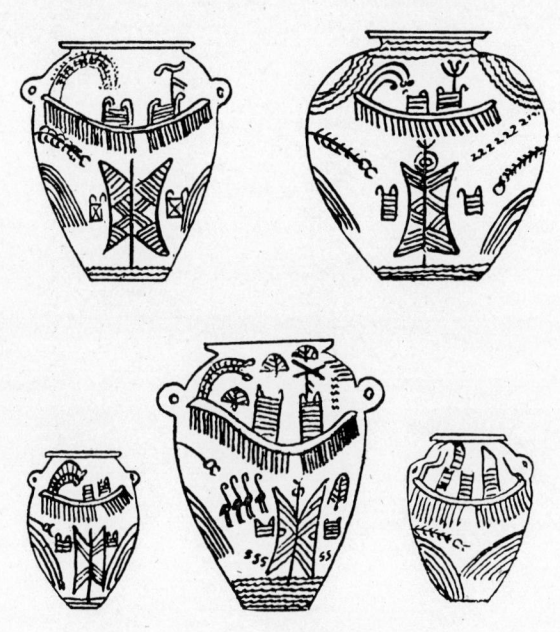

FIG. 31. Decorated pots with boat design.

after s. d. 50, about 4175 b. c., when daggers and chisels of that material are found. Many fresh articles of luxury made their appearance, such as beads of haematite, silver, serpentine, and lapis lazuli; while during the latter half of the period we find gold, amethyst, turquoise, and glazed stone used for this purpose. It is to this time that we would attribute the introduction of cultivated grain and perhaps some of the domesticated animals.

We have seen that not long after the beginning of the Late Predynastic Period, which we are fixing at s. d. 60 or about 3875 b. c., the importation of Syrian ware ceased altogether. Newberry has shown us that at this time a nomadic people, with flocks of sheep and goats, approached the edge of the Delta from the east; these, he thinks, came from the hills of Judaea or the deserts beyond, and introduced into Egypt the cult of the god Anzety. About the same time a Libyan tribe, whom we know later as the Tehennu, advanced to the western margin, and our grain-growers of the Delta found themselves hemmed in by two nomad tribes. The simultaneous arrival in the valley of two sets of steppe-folk seems to show us that at this time the rainfall had become lighter, and that there had occurred one of those recurrent phases of drought, several more of which we shall come across in later centuries,

The eastern nomads, though they brought in sheep and goats, seem to have added little to the culture of the Nile Valley. Goats had not run wild in Africa, and the Barbary sheep, the only native species, has never been tamed. The arrival of these strangers thus brought the knowledge of these domesticated animals to the Nile dwellers, perhaps for the first time. The Tehennu were not long in acquiring some of these, and before the close of the period owned large flocks of sheep. It was the possession of these, perhaps, that inspired them to tame wild asses, which were abundant in the Libyan desert, and they owned large herds of these before the end of the period. They had learned, too, something of agriculture from their North Syrian neighbours, and it is believed that they cultivated the wild olive-trees which they found growing near the southern shore of the Mediterranean.

Meanwhile the Nile-dwellers imitated the Syrian pots, which no longer came to them now that the nomad shepherds had taken possession of the seaport at which they were formerly landed. They developed the pots in their own way, and these became more and more cylindrical in shape as time went on. Other types of pots, some also developed from what were originally foreign models, became more common. Slate palettes continued to be used, though bird and beast forms

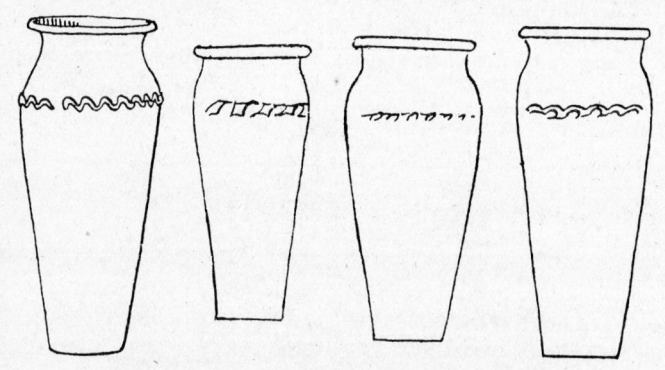

FIG. 32. Wavy-handled pots of native make.

became steadily rarer; ivory combs ceased altogether, though pins of that material were still in use. Harpoons, whether of bone or copper, went out of fashion, and metal was chiefly employed for chisels; beads were made mostly of garnet or porphyry, two materials which had first been introduced during the latter part of the preceding period. Owing to the increasing use of copper the flaking of flint deteriorated, though knives of this material were still in general use.

It will be seen from what has been written that almost every element of culture was introduced from without. The natives of Egypt used wild millet and may later have cultivated it. The

Libyans, after receiving domesticated sheep from Asia, may have tamed the wild ass. The inhabitants of the Arabian Desert may have learned of themselves how to make stone bowls, and the dwellers by the Nile may have discovered independently how to construct a river-boat from bundles of reeds. The other elements of civilization were for the most part introduced from Asia.

At the close of the Late Predynastic Period, about 3400 B.C., there were at least six distinct groups of people inhabiting Egypt, three in the Delta and three in the valley, though the latter had very probably amalgamated by this time. How these various peoples became welded into a nation by Menes, the traditional founder of the first dynasty, must be discussed in a later part.

BOOKS

BREASTED, J. H. *A History of Egypt* (New York, 1912).
FRANKFORT, H. *Studies in Early Pottery in the Near East*, i (London, 1924).
PETRIE, W. M. FLINDERS. *Prehistoric Egypt* (London, 1920).
SMITH, G. ELLIOTT. *The Ancient Egyptians* (London, 1911).
Cambridge Ancient History (London, 1924).
NEWBERRY, P. E. 'Egypt as a Field for Anthropological Research.' The Presidential Address to the Anthropological Section of the British Association (1923).

6

The Dwellers in Mesopotamia

The grain-growers in Mesopotamia were liable to constant raids from the steppe-folk on their margin, especially from the Bedouin who dwelt in the Great Desert of Arabia. Soon some of these came to settle in the plain and established their dominion over portions of it. Later, much later than the times with which we are dealing in this part, a great raid took place which resulted in the foundation of the Kingdom of Babylon; this soon brought nearly the whole of Mesopotamia under Babylonian rule. All this happened rather before 2000 B. C.

The newly arrived invaders from the steppes were barbarians, though they soon acquired, at any rate superficially, the ancient culture of their predecessors in the valley, whom we know as Sumerians. The latter chafed under the foreign yoke, and to remind themselves of their former glory, when various Sumerian cities had in turn held the leadership of a group of free city states, they put together histories of this period of prosperity and compiled lists of the kings and dynasties that had borne rule in former times. Several such lists have come down to us, mostly in a mutilated condition. Until recently the best known of these were some tablets from Nippur, and these agreed in general terms with such accounts as we have received from classical authors, who have quoted extracts from the works of Berosus, a Chaldaean priest who wrote a history of Babylon about 250 B. C.

At the Ashmolean Museum at Oxford is a clay prism, brought back recently from Mesopotamia by Mr. Weld-Blundell, and known as the Weld-Blundell prism or W-B 444.

This contains a more complete list of the kings than do the Nippur tablets, though they are almost identical where comparison is possible. There is still some difference of opinion as to the dates of these kings, and this question we shall discuss in the next part. Here we wish only to point out certain broad features.

These lists all begin with a series of antediluvian monarchs, some giving ten and others eight, and all agreeing in allotting to these kings reigns which in some cases lasted 36,000 and even 72,000 years. Such enormous figures have caused all writers to relegate these antediluvian dynasties, and some, too, which are said to have flourished after the Flood, to the realm of mythology. With this we do not feel disposed to agree, for we have already noted the existence of a culture at Susa, in which wheat was grown and copper used, which came to an end, we believe, owing to a series of violent spring floods. Equally early settlements may have been made in the valleys of the Tigris and Euphrates, though the spade has not yet revealed them.

It is not very many years since the tale of Troy was also relegated to the realm of mythology, from which it was rescued by the labours of Schliemann. The dancing ground in broad Knossos shared the same fate until uncovered by the spade of Sir Arthur Evans. Now these sites, and the civilizations associated with them, have their due place in history, a place by no means remote. According to a recent interpretation of a tablet found not many years ago in Asia Minor, an historical character has now been attributed to Atreus, who as Attarissijas was engaged in fomenting trouble in the Hittite Empire.

Evidence of the existence of some of the early kings of Mesopotamia has come to light during the last few years, and it may not be long before we find remains of the earliest

FIG. 33. The Weld-Blundell Prism.

dynasty to rule after the Flood. We think it not impossible, therefore, that these eight or ten kings actually governed cities or villages by the rivers, though their reigns probably averaged about twenty-five years. We shall assume, therefore, that there were a few settled communities in the plain, lasting for about 200 or 250 years, and that these disappeared for awhile during the period of annual floods, which we believe took place between 4600 and 4400 B. C. This will only bring the earliest settlements here back to 4800 or 4850 B. C., not so early, in fact, as we have placed the first settlement at Susa and the Badarian invasion of Egypt. Of this early culture we know nothing, though we may well believe that grain was cultivated, flax woven, pots made, copper implements used, and perhaps dairy cattle kept. The last king or two are said to have ruled at Šuruppak, which then stood on the banks of the Euphrates, and in some accounts the monarch at the time of the Deluge was named Ziûsuddu or Xisuthros. That he successfully escaped the waters of the Flood in a boat or ark is the theme of a well-known Babylonian epic, and the story has been preserved for us, in a slightly altered guise, in the Book of Genesis.

After the Flood, say the tablets, two dynasties reigned successively at Kish and at Erech, for a period which is given as 26,820 years. In all there were 35 kings, and, if their reigns lasted on an average 25 years each, the time during which these two dynasties flourished would be about 875 years. Thus, if we consider the Flood period as having come to an end about 4400 B. C., the dynasty of Erech ended about 3525 B. C. Working backwards, however, we shall find reason for fixing this date about 3752 B. C. After this came the first dynasty of Ur, about which more is known.

We have already mentioned that Campbell-Thompson found at Abu Sharain, the site of the ancient Eridu, remains

The Dwellers in Mesopotamia

of a prehistoric settlement. Here he discovered numerous chert hoes and ground axe-heads of crystalline rock, together with large quantities of flakes of flint, obsidian and crystal. Besides these there was found a small clay figurine, a number of nails of the same material, and quantities of thin painted pottery. The discovery of corn-grinders and querns shows that

FIG. 34. Back of tablet with account of Flood.

the people to whom these objects belonged cultivated grain. The same kind of pottery was found in small quantities at a number of neighbouring sites, such as Tell-el-Judaidah, Tell-el-Lahm, and Abu Rasain. The same explorer, with H. R. Hall, found similar pottery at Tell el-'Obeid, a few miles from the site of Ur. Similar pottery was found by Dr. Andrae in stratum H at Kalaat Sherkat, the ancient Asshur, and it has been found, too, at Khazneh Tepe, near Kerkûk. Quite recently further sherds of the same ware have been picked up by

Mr. Albright at Tell Zeidân on the east bank of the lower Balîkh river and at Tell es-Semen in the same region. The pottery found on all these sites is very similar and closely resembles that found at Tepeh Musyan, which, it will be remembered, in its upper strata is but a later variety of the ware found in the first settlement at Susa. Both at Abu Sharain and at Tell el-'Obeid the painted ware was found at some depth, lying directly on virgin ground, while the earliest Sumerian remains were lying close to the surface. Quite recently Woolley has found evidence at Ur of a mud settlement more than 20 feet below the pavements of houses which he believes date from the first dynasty. Nowhere on this site did he reach down to a layer with painted pottery.

This civilization is clearly considerably older than the Sumerian culture found on the same site, which, as we shall see, dates from the early years of the first dynasty of Ur, so we may reasonably place the remains of Abu Sharain and Tell el-'Obeid as belonging to the first dynasty of Kish or perhaps earlier. Excavations are at the present time in progress at the site of the latter city, and at any moment the spade may reveal remains dating from its first dynasty.

When we get to the first dynasty of Ur we are on surer ground, for from this time onwards the reigns of the kings are of reasonable length. The first king of the dynasty, it is true, is said to have reigned for eighty years, which is a long reign for the founder of a monarchy, but this is susceptible of a reasonable explanation. When Hall and Woolley were excavating at Tell el-'Obeid in 1922-4 they found remains of a temple erected to the Moon-god Nin-Khursag, and on it a white marble tablet recording that it had been erected by A-an-ni-pad-da, King of Ur, son of Mes-an-ni-pad-da, king of the same city. Now the latter was the founder of the dynasty,

FIG. 35. Objects from Abu Sharain.

whose reign has been given as of eighty years' duration, while A-an-ni-pad-da's name does not occur in the list. It seems likely that the eighty years represents the length of the two reigns taken together.

Langdon first dated the beginning of the first dynasty of Ur at about 4000 B.C., but subsequently reduced this date by fifty-six years. On the other hand, Hall and Woolley would place it at least 500 years later. We propose to return to this subject in our next part, where we shall deal with the question of Egyptian and Mesopotamian chronology; here we will content ourselves with stating that we believe this dynasty to have begun somewhere between 4000 and 3500 B.C.

FIG. 36. Foundation tablet of A-an-ni-pad-da.

At Tell el-'Obeid the explorers found a temple, built of burnt brick, in places resting on a foundation of coursed rubble masonry composed of limestone blocks. The bricks were of the cushion-shaped or plano-convex type usual in early buildings in this region. The building had been adorned with columns made of wood, 'covered with bitumen and encrusted all over with square and triangular tesserae of light red sandstone, black paste, and mother-of-pearl'. There had also been friezes, some inlaid with figures in limestone or shell and one of copper, representing heifers in relief. As cattle formed the chief *motif* in most of these friezes, and in one the cows are represented as being milked from behind, we may conclude that dairying was one of the chief industries at this time at Ur.

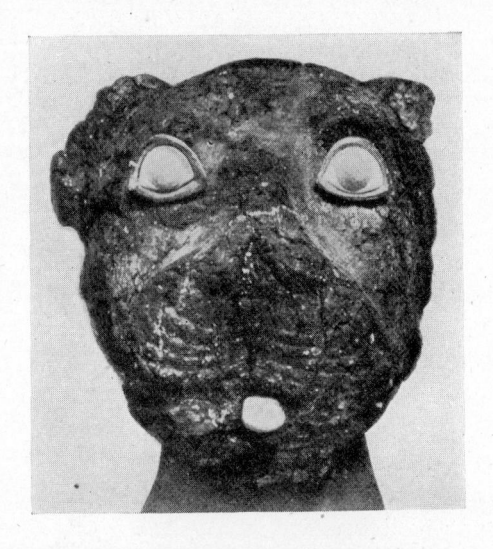

FIG. 37. Copper lions from Tell el-'Obeid.

The proficiency of these people in metal working is shown, not only by the copper frieze already described, but by four copper statues of bulls in the round and two large copper figures of lions, which stood on either side of the entrance. A number of graves were also found, ranging in date from the close of the painted pottery period nearly to 2300 B.C. Some of the earlier of these seem to be contemporary with the temple. The pottery was wheel-made and unpainted and of varied form; copper axes, knives, or daggers were found with stone *coups de poing*, flakes of flint and obsidian, and a few miniature polished stone axe-heads. Some of the metal weapons have recently been shown to contain nearly four per cent. of tin. There were also beads of lapis lazuli and carnelian, and shells containing a soft paste of red haematite or malachite.

At present it is difficult to say anything precise about the events of the remaining period during which the first dynasty of Ur held the leadership among the Sumerian cities. Three kings followed A-an-ni-pad-da, and the last of these, Balulu, died not very long before Menes, the first king of the first dynasty, established himself as monarch over a united Egypt.

Other Sumerian cities, such as Erech, Lagash, and Šuruppak, were already in existence, and it was during this period that the site of Susa was again occupied, this time by a people using polychrome pottery, a ware painted in two colours, red and black, which has also been found at Fara, the ancient Šuruppak, and in the lowest layer at Asshur. Frankfort has identified this polychrome ware as belonging to a people who wore their hair in short pigtails. It has recently been found by Mackay at Jemdet Nasr, about sixteen miles north-east of the site of Kish. This ware has been stated on good authority to recall in many respects some pottery from Cappadocia associated with Hattic or pre-Hittite remains.

Several problems remain to be considered, such as who were the people responsible for the culture at Susa, Tepeh Musyan,

Fig. 38. Polychrome ware from the second settlement at Susa.

Abu Sharain, and Tell el-'Obeid, who were the kings of the first dynasty of Kish, and who were the Sumerians. We need to know also whence these people and their culture came.

Langdon has suggested ' that a great prehistoric civilization spread from Central Asia to the plateau of Iran, and to Syria and Egypt, long before 4000 B.C., and that the Sumerian people, who are a somewhat later branch of this Central Asian people, entered Mesopotamia before 5000 B.C.'; he refers also to the 'intimate relation between the decorative arts of Elam and Anau'. Frankfort has shown conclusively that there is no connexion, at any rate no direct relationship, between the pottery of Anau and that of Susa, and his clear analysis of the remains from the Mesopotamian region shows us that we are dealing with three cultures, probably belonging to three different peoples.

First we have the people with the fine pottery in the earliest settlement at Susa, Abu Sharain, and elsewhere; these grew corn but had no domesticated cattle. Next we have the people with the polychrome ware of Susa II, who wore pigtails; these seem to have been the people afterwards known as Elamites. It is possible that these were a fresh wave of the same people. Lastly we have the Sumerians, who built the temple at Tell el-'Obeid, and whose remains are found in many cities in lower Mesopotamia.

The people of the fine pottery seem to have been hunters from the Iranian plateau, who had learnt the use of grain, pottery, weaving, and copper from some more advanced people, perhaps those dwelling by the upper waters of the Euphrates. In the later stages they had, as we have seen, come under fresh influences from North Syria or Western Anatolia. The pig-tailed people with the polychrome pottery Frankfort brings from North Syria, and his arguments, too long and complicated to summarize here, seem to us absolutely convincing.

Langdon states that the monarchs of the first dynasty of Kish were northern and Semitic. The term Semitic has, as Frankfort has shown, no very distinct meaning at this early

The Dwellers in Mesopotamia

date, but we are prepared to accept Langdon's view that the early inhabitants of Kish came from the north and so to associate them with the pigtailed makers of polychrome pottery.

The Sumerians appear first with the next dynasty, the first of Erech. The Weld-Blundell prism relates that ' At Eanna

FIG. 39. Pigtailed people of Susa II.

Meskemgašer, son of Shamash, was high priest and became king '. Here we seem to have a case of a priestly magistrate, such as were usual under the name of Patesi in later Sumerian cities, proclaiming himself king, apparently with a view to exercising sovereignty over neighbouring city states. It is significant that he claims to be the son of Shamash, the Sun-god. The prism adds, ' Meskemgašer penetrated to the sea and went up into the mountains ', from which we may gather that his warlike expeditions reached the Persian Gulf and the Zagros range. His son, Enmekar, appears to have built Erech and to have become its king during his father's lifetime.

It still remains to decide whence the Sumerians came. We have seen that Langdon's hypothesis does not accord well with the known facts. There is no evidence for an early civilization in Central Asia, nor are the conditions there such as to lead to the cultivation of grain or the working of metal, still less were they so before the ice age had finally passed away. Nor is there any evidence forthcoming of intermediate sites, since that at Anau, to be described in the next chapter, is neither nearly related to nor so early as the first settlement at Susa. Lastly, the precipitous mountain ranges and high arid plateaux which separate Mesopotamia from Central Asia, while not impassable to tribes of wandering hunters or even to pastoral tribes, would have proved severe obstacles to people with a civilization requiring a settled existence.

But the evidence we have cited goes to show that the Sumerian civilization was quite distinct from its two forerunners and arrived after one had disappeared and the other had been established for some centuries at Kish. The Sumerians from the beginning wore a loose robe like a petticoat, or more like a Malay sarong, which seems to indicate that they had come from a hot country, while mother-of-pearl inlay, found in their earliest decorations, points to the possibility that they came from the Persian Gulf.

Hall once suggested that they came from India, and Frankfort thinks this not impossible, and points out that the cattle that they introduced into Mesopotamia are thought to have been of an Indian or at any rate eastern breed. Some authorities have been of opinion that the prehistoric remains found recently by Sir John Marshall at Harappa in the Punjab and

The Dwellers in Mesopotamia

at Mohenjo-daro in Sind may support this view; but this is scarcely possible. Many archaeologists question the connexion between the Indian objects and Mesopotamian culture, and attribute the supposed resemblances to pure chance, while those who believe in a cultural relationship between the two regions admit that the Indian objects resemble Sumerian remains of about 2000 B.C. more nearly than those of earlier days, though seals of Indian origin have been found in Mesopotamia under conditions which, according to Hall, date from 2500 B.C. or earlier. Sir John Marshall has stated recently that he has found several layers beneath the one that he is investigating. While, therefore, we must reject the Indian evidence as having no bearing on Sumerian origins, we cannot rule out the Indian region as a possible original homeland of this people.

But need we go so far as India? Langdon has pointed out that 'the Sumerian legends locate the land of Paradise, where the gods first blessed mankind with manners of civilized life, in Dilmun on the shore of the Persian Gulf'. It is not quite clear on which side of the Gulf Dilmun lay, but the area between the foot of the Iranian plateau and the Gulf is a fertile region, well fitted for the rise of a settled civilization. Besides this there is the plain around Bandar Abbas, on the north side of the Straits of Ormuz, or the slopes of the hills across the Straits as far east as Muscat. But until explorations have been made on either side of the Persian Gulf it is idle to speculate further.

This much seems clear. Between 4000 and 3500 B.C. the Sumerians arrived, probably by sea, at the head of the Persian Gulf, bringing with them for the first time into Mesopotamia herds of dairy cattle, an advanced copper culture, and a habit of decorating objects by means of inlaid slabs of mother-of-pearl and other materials. An old tradition, quoted by Berosus, mentions a being, half fish and half man, who came to Mesopotamia from the sea, bringing elements of culture. It is possible that in this being, Oannes the holy fish, we may see some remembrance of the arrival of the Sumerians.

Whether they brought, too, the art of writing is uncertain. The earliest inscriptions, written in wedge-shaped characters, called cuneiform, upon clay tablets, or cut in the same script upon stone, come from Tell el-'Obeid, and date from the time of the first dynasty of Ur. Earlier and more primitive tablets are known, but, as they lack associations, their dates are uncertain. It may be that these date from the first dynasty of Erech, or it is possible that they go back to the first dynasty of Kish, in which case we must credit the North Syrian or Anatolian culture area with the invention of writing, as well as with other discoveries.

We have made constant reference to the North Syrian or Anatolian culture area, but it is well to remember that its existence is at present a matter of surmise. A number of converging lines of evidence point to its existence, and lead us to suspect that most of the essential elements of civilization developed before 5000 B.C. in some region within 200 miles of Aleppo. No direct evidence of this culture has yet been found, but no serious search for it has been made.

BOOKS

FRANKFORT, H. *Studies in Early Pottery of the Near East*, i (London, 1924).
Cambridge Ancient History, vol. i (London, 1923).
KING, L. W. *A History of Sumer and Akkad* (London, 1910).
DELAPORTE, L. *Mesopotamia* (London, 1925).

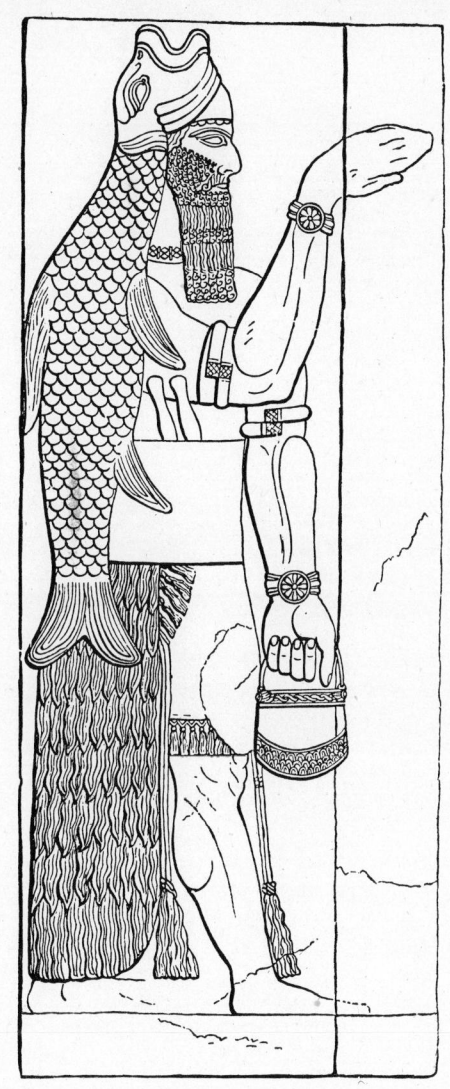

FIG. 40. Oannes.

7
The Isles of the Sea

So far we have been dealing with regions on the continents of Africa and Asia, and we have found evidence of early settlements in Egypt, Mesopotamia, and much of the land lying between them. Although we have found reason for suspecting that the centre of distribution of earliest settlements may have been in or near the north of the Fertile Crescent, no settlements have as yet been found in that province which can be placed earlier than the foundation of the Egyptian kingdom.

On the mainland of Europe also we have no evidence of civilization in the proper sense at so early a date, but in the islands of the Aegean Sea, which form as it were stepping-stones between Asia and Europe, settlements existed, and to them the potter's art at any rate was known.

Our most complete knowledge comes from Crete, and especially from the site of the palace of Knossos, where the excavations carried on for a quarter of a century by Sir Arthur Evans have laid bare a civilization of unsuspected antiquity. Beneath the floor of the palace Evans found a deposit, 6·43 metres in depth, full of fragments of pottery which, from the complete absence of metal, he considers to represent a long neolithic period. In the top 33 cm. the remains are somewhat different, and this layer he has termed sub-neolithic, though we should prefer to call it epi-neolithic; this he has relegated to the beginning of his first Early Minoan Period. The remaining 6·10 metres can safely be considered as dating from before 3400 B.C., and are thought to be neolithic, though they may belong to the early days of metal. That commodity must have been scarce at first, so we may be confident that old implements were remelted rather than thrown away. The knowledge of metal is therefore probably older in many localities than the oldest local layer in which it occurs.

If we are to judge by the rate of accumulation of subsequent deposits, we should consider the beginning of the neolithic period as dating from about 8000 B.C.; in fact, at one time

FIG. 41. Map of Crete and the neighbouring islands.

Evans suggested as early a date as 10,000 B.C. But, as we have seen in the case of Susa, such computations are apt to be misleading, and it would be rash to assume that pottery, and very well-made pottery, was in use in Crete several thousands of years before it was known elsewhere. At present it seems best to offer no suggestions as to the date of the earliest settlement, beyond saying that it must have begun before 4000 B.C. and may well have been in existence as early as 5000 B.C.

Leaving for discussion in the next part the upper or epi-neolithic layer, we may divide the true neolithic period into three, an upper, middle, and lower, of which the upper is considerably

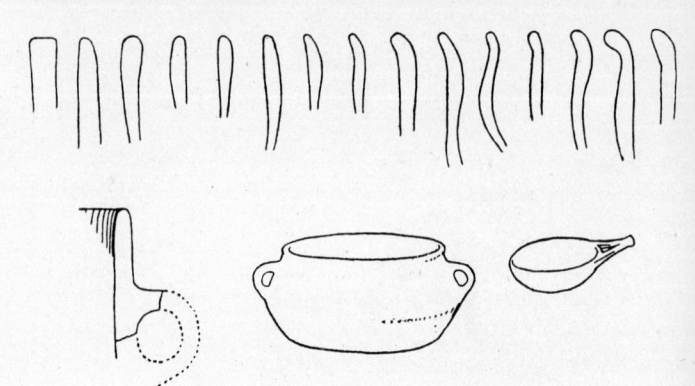

FIG. 42. Neolithic pottery from Magasá.

the shortest. The relative lengths of these three sub-periods can be seen in the following table :

Metres.

Upper Neolithic layer   0·60   plain hand-burnished ware; incised and rippled ware rare.
Middle Neolithic layer   3·00   plain, incised, and rippled ware.
Lower Neolithic layer   2·50   plain ware; incised ware rare.

During the Lower Neolithic sub-period plain pots were made by hand of imperfectly sifted clay, and their surfaces, which had a brownish tint, were more or less burnished. They had wide mouths and flattened bases. Pots decorated with incised geometric designs only appear towards its close. During the Middle Neolithic sub-period incised ware becomes much more abundant, and the incisions are sometimes filled in with white

FIG. 43. Neolithic incised ware. From the Evans Collection in the Ashmolean Museum, Oxford.

or red paint. Some of the plain pots have a rippled surface. The forms of the pots now become much more varied, and we find jugs with handles and trays divided into compartments.

FIG. 44. Neolithic objects from Magasá.

Clay figures of animals and birds make their appearance. The presence of clay spools and spindle-whorls shows us that the arts of spinning and weaving were practised.

Among deposits of this time have been found shells of the *Pectunculus*, which are thought to have had a votive significance.

FIG. 45. Stone axes from Knossos. From the Evans Collection in the Ashmolean Museum, Oxford.

During the Upper Neolithic sub-period both incised and rippled wares die out, while the plain hand-made ware becomes highly burnished, and is sometimes painted with an almost lustreless black glaze slip.

Ground axes of greenstone, serpentine, diorite, jadeite, and

FIG. 46. Neolithic clay idols, Knossos. From the Evans Collection in the Ashmolean Museum, Oxford.

haematite seem to have been used throughout the Neolithic period; these resemble in shape those found in Anatolia. Bone implements are common and of various types; some served as shuttles or needles. During the last phase stone mace-heads, not unlike those found in Mesopotamia and Egypt, make their appearance, which seems to indicate that fresh influences were arriving from the mainland. Such influences had, however, been felt earlier still, for a stud of chrysocolla was found in the Middle Neolithic layer at Knossos, and this closely resembles some recently found in early Sumerian graves at Ur.

Perhaps the most interesting feature of this period is the presence of a number of clay figurines. Most of these represent a seated female figure, with the head and arms imperfectly modelled. They bear some resemblance to figures found in

FIG. 47. Predynastic Egyptian bowl, from Knossos. From the Evans Collection in the Ashmolean Museum, Oxford.

other islands and on the Asiatic mainland, and are thought to represent the Mother Goddess apparently worshipped in early days in Anatolia. Similar figures are found much farther afield, and the cult may have been carried by Cretan mariners.

From the other islands of the Aegean we have no direct evidence of civilization at this early date; at any rate no settlements or graves have been found which can with certainty be dated before 3400 B.C. On the other hand, there is much indirect evidence. Small tools and points of obsidian have been found plentifully in the neolithic deposits of Crete and less commonly in predynastic graves in Egypt, while the only source of supply for this material in the Eastern Mediterranean is the island of Melos, whence large stocks of this substance were shipped a few centuries later.

Again, to hollow out bowls from hard stones emery would have been required, both in Crete and Egypt; this mineral seems to have been found in the island of Naxos and near the coast of Asia Minor. Since obsidian is found among some of the earliest neolithic deposits at Knossos, we must suppose that a culture, almost if not quite as advanced as that of Crete, existed in other Aegean islands from an early time, and the resemblance of many of the items of these cultures to stray finds from Asia Minor justifies Evans's statement that the earliest ' culture of Crete (representative of the Aegean Islands in general) may be regarded as an insular offshoot of an extensive Anatolian province '.

That the people were seafarers is obvious from the above statements, but we have no information as to the form of their boats. Models of boats have, however, been found in graves of a slightly later date both in Crete and in the Cyclades. The wide range of some of their early products seems to indicate that the voyages of the Aegean mariners were of long duration; for obsidian implements have been found as far west as Italy and even beyond, and some think that these came from Melos, though obsidian occurs in the West Mediterranean. Pottery resembling in many ways that of Neolithic Crete has been found in South Italy, Sicily, Sardinia, the island of Pianosa, and the Ligurian caves, while the cult of the *Pectunculus* shell is even more widely spread.

Though few remains of dwellings of this period have yet been found, we know that sometimes the early Cretans built houses of stone. At Magasá, near Palaikastro, Dawkins found the

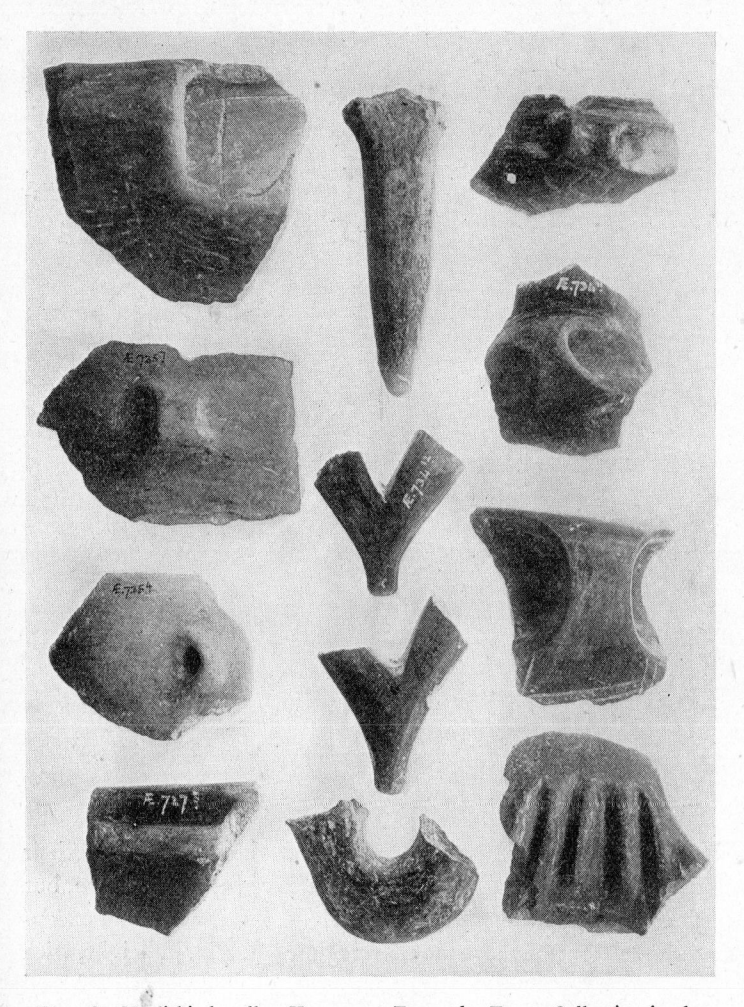

FIG. 48. Neolithic handles, Knossos. From the Evans Collection in the Ashmolean Museum, Oxford.

lower part of a building, composed of a single course of undressed limestone blocks. The building, which was approximately rectangular in plan, consisted of two rooms, a small entrance chamber and a larger one within.

Unfortunately no graves of this period have yet been dis-

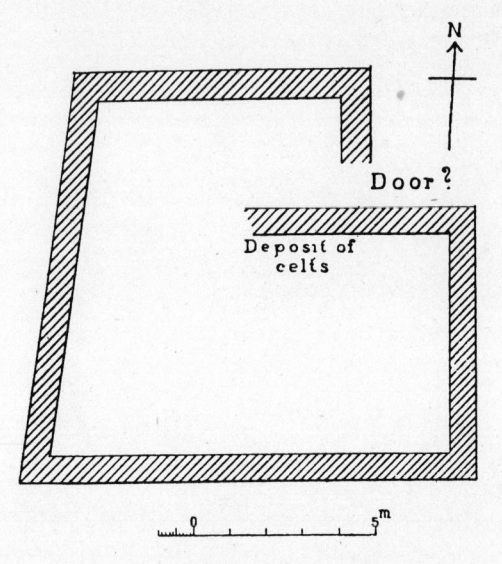

FIG. 49. Neolithic house at Magasá.

covered, so we are unable to say how they disposed of their dead. We also have no direct evidence of their racial type, but since graves of the subsequent period contain with one exception skeletons of short men, averaging 5 ft. 4 in. in height, with long narrow skulls, and since the proportion of men with broad skulls increases in subsequent periods, we may conjecture that the majority of these earliest inhabitants of Crete were small slender dark-skinned people with long and narrow heads. On

The Isles of the Sea

the other hand, since the majority of the cultural elements that we have described seem to have come from Anatolia, where the people are taller but with broader and shorter heads, we can well imagine that folk of the Anatolian type formed a part of the population.

We have seen that of the various items that went to make up primitive civilization the people of Crete knew the potter's art

FIG. 50. Clay figures of oxen. From the Evans Collection in the Ashmolean Museum, Oxford.

and had developed some skill in the textile industry. On the other hand, we lack evidence of their knowledge of metal and the art of writing. Nothing has yet been found to tell us whether or no they were accustomed to cultivate grain or whether they kept any domesticated animals. On the latter point we may conjecture that they kept goats, for these animals are probably native to the island; perhaps they kept sheep also, for a wild sheep, the moufflon, ran wild in the island.

Clay figures of oxen may also indicate that they kept cattle. On their sea-faring powers we have already enlarged. It seems probable that the civilization in the other islands of the Aegean was on much the same level.

BOOKS

EVANS, Sir A. J. *The Palace of Minos at Knossos, Crete* (London, 1921).
CHILDE, V. GORDON. *The Dawn of European Civilization* (London, 1925).
BURROWS, RONALD M. *The Discoveries in Crete* (London, 1907).
HAWES, C. H. and H. B. *Crete the Forerunner of Greece* (London, 1909).

8

On the Edge of the Steppes

To the east of the Caspian Sea lies the province of Russian Turkestan, a region of stony desert and in places grassy steppe-land. To the south the mountains of the Kopet Dagh range rise abruptly from a few hundred to more than six thousand feet above sea-level, and divide the steppe-land of Turkestan from the Iranian plateau. The mountains are thickly wooded, except on the highest points; coniferous trees reach nearly to the summit, below them is a belt of deciduous trees, while near the bottom flourish evergreens of types found in the Mediterranean basin. Between the wooded mountain and the dry steppe or desert lies a very narrow fertile belt, on the lowest foot-hills of the range, watered by streams which rise in the heights but dry up and disappear after passing a few miles into the plain. Along this narrow belt of fertile soil runs the Transcaspian railway past Askabad to Merv, and within a few miles of its track are to be found, not only whatever modern settlements exist, but such traces of occupation as have survived from the past.

Along this fertile belt may be seen a number of long, low mounds, especially in the section between Bami and Dushak. These have been briefly noted by Casson, who has observed, too, a number of similar mounds between Tiflis and Tatlu, in the valley of the Kara, which runs south of the Caucasus

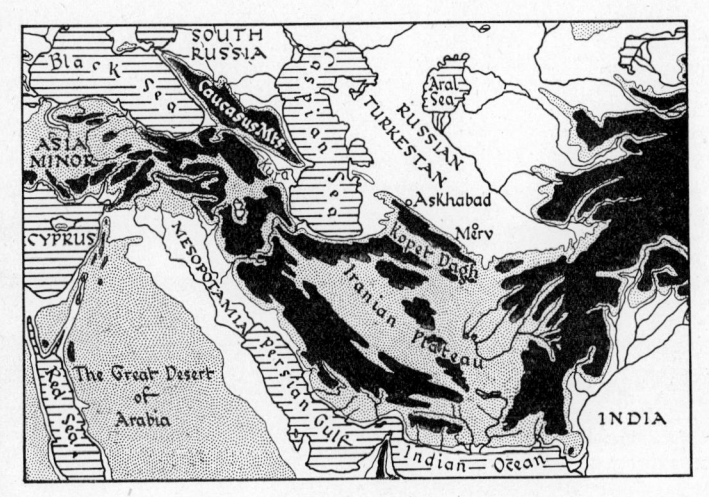

FIG. 51. Map of the Caspian region.

mountains into the Caspian Sea. These mounds, known there as *kurgans*, may sometimes be large barrows or burial mounds, but the majority are much too big to have been erected for that purpose, and are thought to be the sites of villages that have long ago disappeared. That two of them are certainly such sites has been made clear to us by the researches of Mr. Raphael Pumpelly, which we are going to describe.

Villages in early days often consisted of mud huts or huts

built of sun-dried bricks, such as may be seen to-day in the Nile Delta; some may have been constructed of wattle and daub. Such huts were not calculated to last long and must have been rebuilt at frequent intervals, and each new hut would have been built on the ruins of its predecessor. Thus by degrees the level of the village rose above the surrounding plain, as may be seen in the Nile Delta at the present day.

Primitive man is not usually a cleanly animal, and his huts, used mainly to sleep in, were seldom if ever cleaned out, and if to the ordinary rubbish and the remains of his meals we add the mud brought in on his feet from his fields, we can well believe that the mound would grow at a great pace. At one site, the walled city of Anau, abandoned during the nineteenth century, Pumpelly calculated that the level had risen at the rate of 2 ft. 3 in. a century during the last four hundred years, while during the previous nine centuries, when the people had, perhaps, been still less clean, the rate was more than 2 ft. 6 in. In still earlier times we can well believe that the accumulation during each century was greater still.

The site of the abandoned city of Anau lies about twenty miles east-south-east of Askabad, and about a mile west of these ruins lie two mounds or kurgans, one, known as the North Kurgan, forty feet high, about half a mile south of the Transcaspian railway, the other, the South Kurgan, fifty feet high, about a mile still farther to the south. These mounds were first noticed and described by Mr. Raphael Pumpelly, a retired American engineer, who was exploring parts of Central Asia in 1903 on behalf of the Carnegie Institution of Washington. He returned on behalf of the same institution in 1904, accompanied by a number of American experts and Dr. Hubert Schmidt of Berlin, who had been trained as an archaeologist by Dr. Dörpfeld during his excavations on the site of Troy.

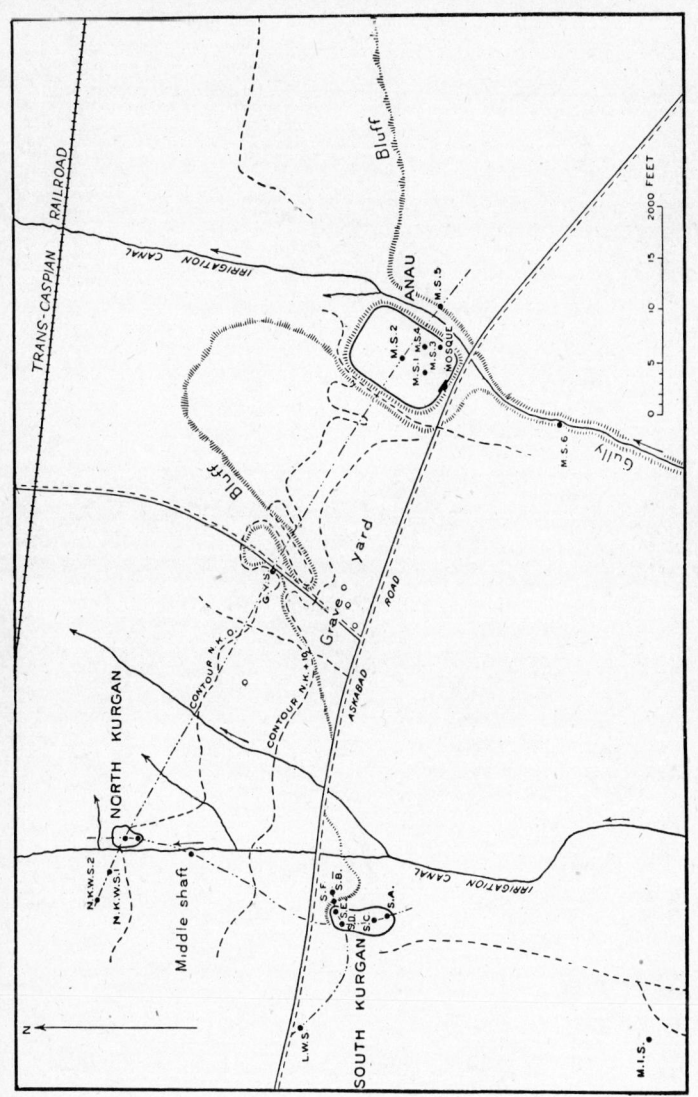

FIG. 52. Map of the Anau oasis.

The exploration of the mounds was most carefully carried out by Dr. Schmidt, and it was found that they belonged to different periods. The North Kurgan was found to be the older, and, though the occupation of the site seems to have been continuous, Dr. Schmidt has relegated the remains to two periods, which he has called Anau I and Anau II.

The lowest culture in the South Kurgan was clearly more developed than that found in the highest layer of the North Kurgan, and the pottery found there, though not differing widely from that of the other mound, led Schmidt to conclude that a period of uncertain length had elapsed between the abandonment of the North Kurgan and the foundation of the earliest settlement which led to the formation of its southern neighbour. The South Kurgan contained two very different cultures, the uppermost of fairly recent date, so that it was clear that the site had been abandoned for some centuries and then reoccupied by another people with a different mode of life. These two cultures are known as Anau III and Anau IV.

Pumpelly has endeavoured to date these cultures by calculations based on the time it must have taken for these mounds to accumulate, and the rate of the deposition of the loess on the plain around. His figures are:

Anau IV   about 500 B.C.   Anau II   6000–5200 B.C.
Anau III   5200–2200 B.C.   Anau I   before 8000–6000 B.C.

On the other hand, Schmidt, who has based his estimates on certain resemblances to cultures elsewhere, gives the following provisional figures:

Anau IV   1000–500 B.C.   Anau II   —————— B.C.
Anau III   ———1000 B.C.   Anau I   before 2000——— B.C.

It is clear that the dates suggested by Pumpelly are greatly exaggerated, for were we to accept them we should be placing the whole of the civilization of the North Kurgan earlier than the first settlement at Susa and the introduction of the Badari culture into Egypt. On the other hand, Schmidt's dates are far from satisfactory, for he allows no interval between cultures III and IV, and compresses the first three cultures, including the gap between II and III, into the space of less than two thousand years.

Frankfort dismisses Pumpelly's dates and the relationship between the wares of Anau and those of Susa suggested by some writers, but has deferred a full consideration of the chronology of the Anau pottery and its cultural connexions to the second part of his work, which has not appeared as we write. We are disposed to think, for reasons which will be given in full in a later part, that the settlement at the South Kurgan, Anau III, began not later than about 2400 B.C. and perhaps a century earlier; it may have lasted for nine hundred or a thousand years. What length of time elapsed between the abandonment of the village on the North Kurgan and the establishment of the fresh settlement is not clear, and any estimate must be in the nature of guesswork. We are inclined to suggest that the North Kurgan deposits were growing between 3900 and 2750 B.C., though the period might have been shorter and the dates more recent. If we accept these dates provisionally, and assume that the kurgan deposits accumulated at an even rate, we must assume that the earliest culture in the mound, that termed by Schmidt Anau I, lasted from about 3900 to 3300 B.C., and so fell within the period of which we are treating in this part.

The people of the first settlement made pottery in great quantities, and this they painted, ornamenting it with geometrical designs. Though they were ignorant of the potter's wheel, and their pots had no handles, and were never incised or glazed, it is Frankfort's opinion that the forms of the vessels show that the art was not young, and that it had been introduced from elsewhere in a fairly developed stage.

These people built for themselves rectangular houses of

FIG. 53. Pottery from the first culture of Anau.

sun-dried bricks, but they had not yet learnt to burn their bricks in a kiln. For tools they used straight-edged flakes of flint and awls of the same material and of bone; like the early Egyptians, Cretans, and the dwellers in Mesopotamia they had mace-heads of stone. On the other hand, no axes of stone or metal were found, nor spear-heads or even arrow-heads of any kind.

The presence of corn-grinders shows that they prepared grain for food, and in some of the potsherds, from the lowest layer of the mound, were impressions of the husks of both wheat and barley. Though it is clear from this that from the first they were cultivators of grain, they had no domesticated

FIG. 54. Flint implements from Anau I.

animals during the first few centuries. For meat they depended on the chase, and they seem to have hunted cattle, sheep, gazelles, deer, horses, foxes, wolves, and wild boars. How they killed their quarry is uncertain, for no remains of weapons of the chase were found, nor is there any evidence that they possessed dogs until the second period. After a time they domesticated a long-horned breed of cattle, pigs, and horses, and, successively, two breeds of sheep, but no remains of goats or camels were found in these layers.

The early settlers at Anau were in a state of civilization very similar to that of the first dwellers at Susa, though they had no dogs and much less copper, and it seems clear that their pottery was of an entirely different type, in spite of the claims which have been made for a relationship between the two. On the other hand, not long after their settlement at Anau they became acquainted with certain domestic animals, and these,

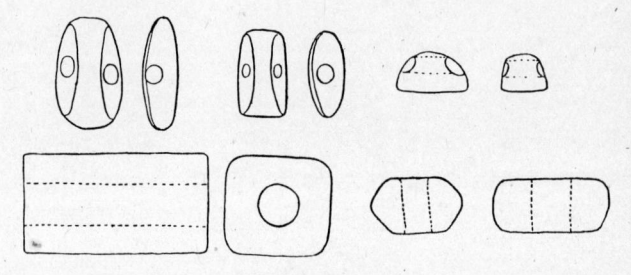

FIG. 55. Copper objects from Anau I.

or some of them, we can well believe they acquired from their neighbours on the steppes to the north. The domestication of the sheep, which is a mountain animal, they may have learnt from the hill tribes to the south, or, perhaps, having acquired cattle they may have tamed the sheep themselves.

Frankfort is probably correct in believing that the potter's art reached Anau from somewhere in Anatolia, and it may well be that the other arts were derived from the same source; if so, they came ultimately from that centre which gave rise to the cultures of Egypt and Mesopotamia. It is likely enough that the Anau kurgans are not the only or even the earliest settlements in this part of the world, for, as we have seen, there are many similar mounds at the northern foot of the Kopet Dagh and others of the same type at the southern foot of the Caucasus. Until some of these have been explored, and until more is known of early settlements in Asia Minor, it will be impossible to place the culture of Anau in its true relation to early civilization elsewhere.

BOOKS

PUMPELLY, R. *Explorations in Turkestan* (Washington, 1908).
FRANKFORT, H. *Studies in Early Pottery of the Near East*, i (London, 1924), and the second part when it appears.

9
Peoples, Nations, and Languages

THE names of peoples in ancient records present a bewildering problem, for they represent groups of many kinds. Some of these groups are warriors, aggregated together for an invasion or crusade, while others are agglomerates of wandering tribes; others again are the settled cultivators of a region, sometimes independent, often in servitude to an aristocracy of conquerors, while there are trading groups and groups with a common religion. Moreover the names of peoples were apt to change from time to time. Thus a conquered group might lose its name and become absorbed into the conquering group, perhaps with some attendant change of language or religion; small outlying groups might be drawn into the orbit of a larger one, adopting its language, it may be, and taking some share in its economic life. These are but a few of the methods by which a people may be said to dissolve away or by which an agglomerate of elements, perhaps distinct in origin, may come to form a ' people '.

Once we have realized this great mutability of human groupings, we are prepared for inevitable difficulty in determining the races to which peoples may have belonged either wholly or in part. When many persons resemble one another very closely in their physical characters and are distinguished by these characters from their neighbours, we refer to their resemblances as race characters. A group of such persons we may call a race, in the belief that the individuals concerned are the descendants of a few ancestors, who formed a group distinguished by these characters. There is, however, need for caution, for it seems possible that sometimes an intrusive element may introduce some physical characters which tend to appear in most or all of the offspring, even if only one parent possessed them. All this shows us how difficult it is to identify the race with the social group. The difficulties are increased by the loose way in which the term 'race' is sometimes used.

Language is one of the prime factors of social life, for it is necessary that the members of a social group should be able to understand one another. Languages may, however, be altered unconsciously, though it is difficult to change them deliberately. Unconscious alteration is often a slow change, like that which is now at work among the English-speaking peoples; this change unfortunately is now deepening the cleft between English and the speech of English origin in use on the other side of the Atlantic. We have only to think of the latter to realize that the North American language group in question is composed of peoples whose mother tongues are of Romance, British, German, Norse, Slavonic, and other origins.

It is dangerous to argue that a language group, even in antiquity, belonged to any one race type. Nevertheless, the making of sounds depends to some extent on physical characters; thus it is easier for people with long upper lips than for those with the upper lip short to make the *p*-sound clearly. It may well be, therefore, that in very early times a social group was both a group with community of descent, or as we should call it a race-group, and a group with common speech, that is to say a language-group. This simple linkage of race and language with the social group can, at most, have belonged only to very early times. Admixture came soon enough.

We have refrained so far from using the term 'nation', which we should be inclined to define as a group bound together by some common measure of sentiment and attachment, often arising from common experiences, usually of defence. How far it would be justifiable to call the Egyptian population of the Old Kingdom a nation, or to use that term for the Sumerians of the same centuries or the Hittites of a later date, might be disputed indefinitely. These are, at all events, the ancient social groups best known to us that approach most nearly to the standard of national units.

Let us consider first what we know of racial types in the period under consideration. The great majority of the people inhabiting North Africa, Arabia, and Persia at the present time is long-headed and usually has an olive to red-brown skin. The people vary among themselves to some extent, and those on the Asiatic side in particular often have more conspicuous noses than their fellows in Africa. Some individuals among the Shawiya of the Aures Massif in Algeria are fairer in colouring than the majority of the natives of North Africa, and suggestions have been made to the effect that they are descendants of ancient intruders. Elliot Smith has shown from an examination of a great number of burials that the predynastic people of Upper Egypt were mostly of the same type as now, and it is likely that this is true for the whole region. We know also that the majority of skulls dating from the latter part of the Old

Stone Age of Europe is long-headed, and several suggestions have been made concerning the survival of these old types in modern populations, suggestions that cannot be effectively opposed.

The probability is that, with the drying of the Sahara and Arabia, following the northward drift of the storm zone in the last part of the Ice Age, peoples pressed towards the coasts and towards river valleys like those of the Nile and of the Tigris and Euphrates. Doughty calls North-West Arabia a highland steppe, and it differs little in parts from a fully marked desert; it is more than probable that it dried rather later than did the Sahara.

On the whole we may picture a long-headed population, with olive to red-brown skins and wavy hair, ranging throughout the desert and steppe-lands of North Africa, Arabia, and Persia and their borders. These, from their early history on the grass-lands that became the wastes of the Sahara, Arabia, and Persia, may be called the Southern Steppe-folk, or the 'Brown Race' in Elliot Smith's terminology, though the latter name may at times include their long-headed relatives farther east, especially in Central and South India, as well as migrants thence to the East Indies and beyond.

Elliot Smith thus describes them: Long-headed, dark-skinned people, with scanty face-hair save for a chin tuft in the male, bodies slender, long, narrow and often 'ill-filled' skulls with eyebrow ridges poorly developed or absent. The forehead is narrow, vertical, smooth, and often slightly bulging; the occiput is very prominent at the back of the head. The orbits may be either low or circular and have thin margins, the cheek-bones are flattened at the sides and the cheeks are correspondingly narrow. The nose is usually small, rather broad and flattened at its bridge. The chin is pointed and the jaw rather weak. Elliot Smith has shown abundantly that, from the days

Peoples, Nations, and Languages 123

of the early dynasties of Ancient Egypt, aliens of other type had come in to the Lower Nile region at least. Among them were broad-headed individuals, presumably from Asia Minor.

The Brown Race in this broad sense must not be considered as uniform everywhere. Though long-headedness is very general, the degree of it varies a great deal, and so does the grade of skin colour, which ranges from olive to almost black. There are also other differences. Inhabitants of warm areas, especially

FIG. 56. Hamite and Semite.

if they live a settled life, are apt to mature more quickly than do peoples who move a great deal or who live under colder conditions, especially if the latter have to stand a good deal of exposure to a cold season. Those who mature later generally have not only a higher average stature but also a more marked profile, and it is this difference which seems to mark off the inhabitants of Arabia, with their sharper profile, from the native peoples of North Africa. The people of the hills and plateaux around the basin deserts of Persia seem to have received elements from farther north and their skins are rather less coloured. They are named, for convenience, Iranians.

It has been shown that Solutrean-like implements, much later in date than the Solutrean period in Europe, have been found at Susa and with the Badarian culture in Egypt. From this it may reasonably be argued that some people from farther north in Asia penetrated at an early date not only into Persia but even as far as the Nile or beyond it westwards.

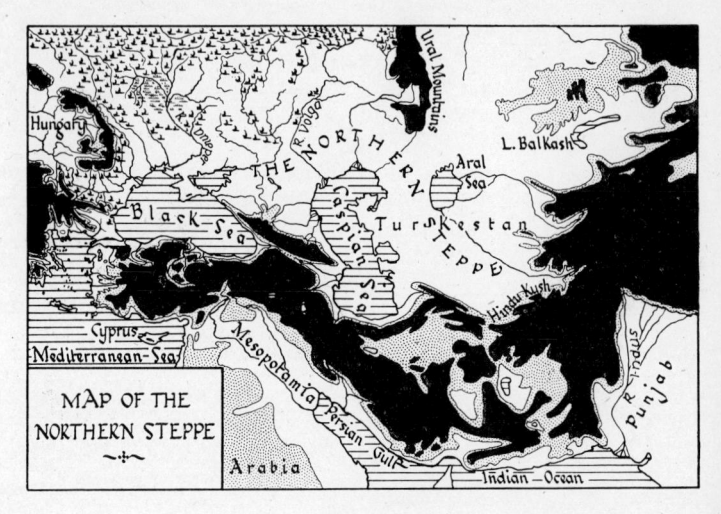

Fig. 57.

We have seen that, with the advance of the forest over large regions north of the Alps, the Solutrean hunters of horses and other big game retreated with the latter, probably to the steppe which stretched and still stretches from the Dnieper around the north of the Caspian Sea to the Hindu Kush. A small belt of steppe, or steppe with occasional trees, was left farther west where fine-grained loess soil or the porosity of the country rock hindered tree growth, and along this comparatively open belt can be traced the eastward spread of the Final Capsian

Ofnet

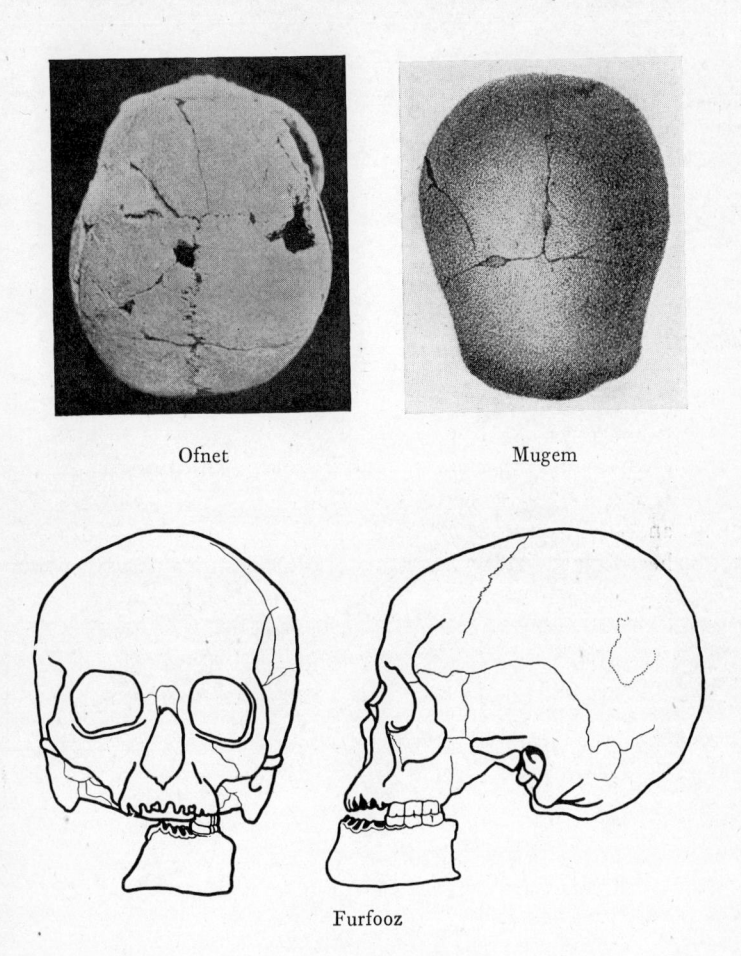

Mugem

Furfooz

Fig. 58. Broad skulls from Ofnet, Mugem, and Furfooz.

invaders, who apparently also reached the great steppes just mentioned. It seems likely that their descendants have been ever since an element of various populations living near this belt. The skulls from Solutré, the age of which is still rather uncertain, tell of a people on the whole rather less long-headed than the Southern Steppe-folk, but including quite long-headed elements. On the whole they ran taller than the North African peoples, and it is said that the men of Predmost were in some cases quite tall. A few human remains from Anau are of long-headed types, which Sergi and others have thought to be near the Mediterranean or Southern Steppe type, and there is no doubt that early Northern and Southern Steppe-folk had great resemblances each to the other.

From the period of transition between the Old Stone Age and the New Stone Age we get unmistakable evidence of broad-headed people at Ofnet in Bavaria, at Furfooz in Belgium, and even at Mugem on the Tagus. It seems likely on the whole that this element was introduced from outside, rather than that it was aboriginal on the plains of Europe north of the mountain zone. We thus, at least provisionally, think of the European and Eurasiatic plains as peopled in early times chiefly by long-headed descendants of men of the latter part of the Old Stone Age, with rough features. These still survive in out-of-the-way corners. More generally, as their homes and cooking improved, their jaws and jaw muscles became less pronounced, and their faces took on a milder aspect. These long-heads usually, if we may judge from their modern descendants, had pale skins and well-marked profiles; we may call them the Northern Steppe-folk, but we must remember that the Final Capsian spread may have brought along with it North African elements. One may picture these people at first as food-collectors; later on, perhaps, doing a little rough cultivation; but in the great steppe, drawn more and more towards the work of following, guiding, and controlling flocks and herds, and so becoming the nomad herdsmen of the ancient grass-lands.

Objection may be raised to the term Steppe-folk, for with both the Northern and Southern groups were early associated coastal fishers and Nile-dwellers, and many others who were by no means Steppe-folk. The steppes, however, both in the north and the south were nevertheless sources of men, exported to the lands round about them, especially when drought followed a period of prosperity in the grass-land.

The Northern and Southern Steppe-folk of early times were separated by a great mountain zone, consisting of the Alps, the Balkan Peninsula, Asia Minor, Armenia, and the Caucasus. Asia Minor and the Alpine zone in Europe are almost everywhere characterized nowadays by a broad-headed population, and there is every indication that this population has been established here for a very long time. The Hittite monuments of 1400 B.C. show quite clearly the present-day types, and Hittites on some ancient Egyptian monuments are distinguished from Semites and Egyptians by their paler skins as well as by their features. If a physical type has persisted through all vicissitudes between 1400 B.C. and A.D. 1900 it is likely to go still farther back in the story of the region.

In Europe, comparison of the physical types of different regions shows that types linked with those just mentioned as existing in Asia Minor are found in the western portion of the Balkan Peninsula. Both have the head very short from front to back and usually it is high, often practically domed. The profile is usually very pronounced and the nose generally projects forward to an extent almost unknown elsewhere. Where nutrition is not too poor, this type is often quite tall. On the other hand, the Alpine zone proper, in Switzerland and the Central Massif of France, shows as one of its most characteristic types a man with broad rounded head, without any striking development of nose or profile, and with a rather short stature and thick-set build. Observations regarding peoples in and near the Carpathian mountain arc suggest that modifications of both these varieties of round-heads occur there. It is possible to see links between the broad-heads of the Pamirs and other Asiatic regions and those of Alpine Europe, but the Asia Minor type of broad-head is not characteristic either of the Pamirs or of Alpine Europe.

The zone of highland from the Pyrenees through the Alps, Carpathians, Balkan Peninsula, Asia Minor, Armenia, the Pamirs, and onwards to Manchuria seems to be largely a belt of broad-heads, and it is likely that the broad-heads so characteristic of the highland zones of America, like all the native peoples of that continent, are descendants of migrants who moved thither long ago around North-East Asia. Various speculations have been made as to the origin of broad-headedness, either in relation to a highland environment direct or to the kinds of food and methods of food mastication usual in such a region. It seems best to avoid this type of argument, though one may point out that in early times the infants who had to hold and tear ill-cooked flesh with their teeth were likely to diverge in growth from those who chewed grain, especially if the latter was softened for their benefit. One may also suggest that the nose does seem to grow rather differently in different regions, and there can be little doubt that profile and head-form have subtle and complex interrelations. Many other points would need to be brought into a complete discussion, but the matter has not yet reached that stage.

However broad-headedness may have come into existence in modern types of man, there can be little doubt as to the dis-

FIG. 59. Hittite and Anatolian types.

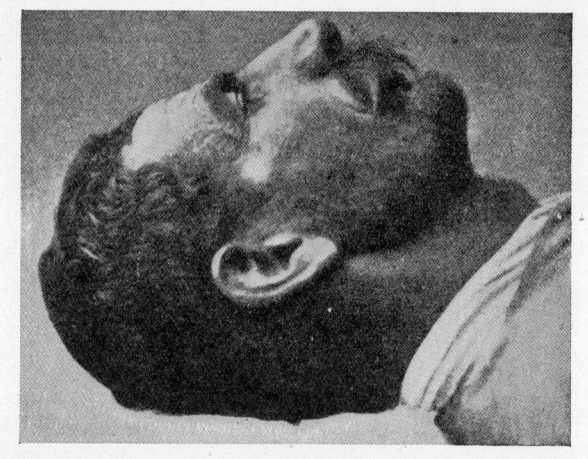

tinction, which reveals itself in ever so many physical characters, between the truly broad-headed and the truly long-headed types, and especially the long-headed hunters and artists of the Aurignacian and Magdalenian stages. The broad-headed types of the French Central Massif and the Alps share with many of the broad-heads of the Pamir region a round ovoid outline of the head, which is not very high; they are, however, separated

FIG. 60. Western Alpine types.

by the tall broad-heads of Asia Minor and parts of the Balkan Peninsula, who have the head very short, flat at the back, and in many cases very high. It is possible that this latter type is a further development of broad-headed character over and above that shown by the former, but as to the place of origin of either one can hardly even speculate as yet.

We may hope for some further light on racial character as excavations in Mesopotamia develop. Recently at Kish, in a Sumerian palace of the Bronze Age, several skulls have been found, mostly in a broken condition. From an examination

Peoples, Nations, and Languages

and reconstruction of several of these, Buxton has shown that six out of the seven are distinctly long-headed and that, in the three cases in which it was possible to measure the height, this measurement was conspicuously great, giving the skull vault a keel shape. This suggests that we are dealing with representatives of the older elements in Elliot Smith's Brown Race or our Southern Steppe-folk. One skull is quite different and

FIG. 61. Ur-Nina and his family.

belongs to a markedly broad-headed type with orbits set obliquely as they are in some Sumerian representations, though the details are by no means Mongoloid. It seems likely that this broad-head has connexions with Asia Minor.

It seems probable that in places like the Fertile Crescent there was from very early times an admixture of types that may well have included:

(*a*) Survivors of more or less aboriginal men of the types prevalent in Aurignacian and succeeding times; long-headed, dark, bony people with strong brows and large cheek-bones and, very likely, broad noses.

(*b*) Various Southern Steppe-folk, some allied to the types inhabiting the Nile valley as described by Elliot Smith, and some with sharper profiles and stronger growth as indicated above.

(*c*) Some Northern Steppe-folk, perhaps lighter in colouring, but long-headed like the rest.

(*d*) Mediterranean coastal peoples, some allied to (*b*) and some probably allied to (*e*).

(*e*) Broad-headed individuals both of the Asia Minor and of the Pamir varieties.

The people of the first settlement at Susa are believed to have been long-headed. The Sumerians appear to be of mixed origin, as one would expect. The Anau people are little known, but seem to have been long-headed.

It is to the mixture of people of different type, training, and outlook around the hill borders of the Fertile Crescent that we are inclined to attribute the beginnings of agriculture, pottery, dairy kine, as distinct from the great herds of the steppe, and probably of the use of metal. The Northern Steppe-folk did not for ages take kindly to agriculture, and the spread of agriculture into Europe seems to have been largely along the Alpine and sub-Alpine zone, apart from what may have occurred around the Mediterranean coasts.

The suggestion that peoples and traditions mingled in the Fertile Crescent is of great importance, for it has often been argued, especially by the late Dr. Rivers, that the establishment of contacts between peoples with different training and equipment produces new ideas and liberates initiative. We are creatures of habit, and, if left to ourselves, we are apt to get into a groove. Contact with persons of different outlook forces us out of this and is likely to make us reflect upon the taboos of the society in which we have been brought up, especially if they seem to impose upon us penalties and restrictions not experienced by the people of different outlook. Very often, though not always, there follows a weakening of taboo and thus a growth of initiative, which may strike out in what are practically new directions. The amount of initiative connected with great centres of intermixture in medieval Europe like Flanders and Florence is well known and may be used by way of example.

In the matter of language, as in that of race characters, mountains and difficult hill country are typical refuges of cast-up remnants of the far past. Basque in the Pyrenees, Romansch, Ladin, and Frioul in and near the Alps, and the medley of tongues in the Caucasus are cases in point. The languages of the lowlands encroached on those of the valleys in the hill country, for the latter keep apart and diverge still farther from one another through difficulties of intercommunication. Often, too, there is no centre where a standard speech can develop by the paring off of dialectal eccentricities and new words can be properly naturalized. We should, therefore, not expect to find marked spreads of language from hills to plains even in the past, for then as now it was the plains-folk who made most frequent and varied contacts, and who thus acquired a widespread medium of speech, shorn of some of the extravagant peculiarities one generally finds in small localities. It seems most profitable at present to think of language-families associated with the Northern and with the Southern Steppe-folk, and of their influence, especially that of the language of the former, on the hill and mountain country from Armenia to the Pyrenees.

Over the greater part of the Southern Steppe-lands Arabic is now spoken, but this is of relatively recent introduction. The Kabyles and the Shawiya of Algeria, and the Tuaregs of the Sahara, speak allied tongues, which, with numerous others, are collectively known as Hamitic, and are generally considered to be the descendants of the original tongue of the Sahara region. Throughout the steppes and deserts of Arabia languages are spoken which are collectively known as Semitic; to the same group belonged Babylonian, Assyrian, and Hebrew. The language of Ancient Egypt seems to have been Hamitic at first, but to have become partly Semitized as time passed. We are inclined to think that the arrival of fresh elements from the Arabian desert between Thebes and the Red Sea with stone jars at the beginning of the Middle Predynastic Period, as well as the frequent arrival of nomads in the Delta of the Nile, may be taken as types of influences from Semitic lands upon Hamitic Egypt. It is probable that Hamitic and Semitic languages diverged from a common source.

The problem of the languages of the Northern Steppe-folk has long engaged attention. As early as the closing years of the eighteenth century students of languages had realized that nearly all forms of European speech and some of those spoken in Asia were allied. From similarities of words in various languages it is argued that the people who are presumed to have spoken the mother tongue of the whole group knew the horse, cow, sheep, pig, and dog, and were accustomed to wheat and barley and to their cultivation; they had also common words for the numerals. The horse suggests that their original homeland lay in some part of the Northern Steppe-lands, and this suggestion is supported by detailed comparative study of the languages of Europe and of some in Asia. The Teutonic, some Celtic and the Latin and Greek groups, as well as the Tocharian language of parts of Turkestan, use frequently the sounds indicated in the English convention by the letters *k*, *g*, and *gh*. These sounds are replaced by sibilants in Sanskrit and its Indian offspring, in Persian as far back as it is known in writing, and in Armenian, though that language has other elements as well; this use of sibilants is also found in the Slavonic and in the old Baltic tongues. The whole group of languages has common grammatical features and may be said to possess on the whole a more regular scheme of grammar than is found in other languages. On the whole this family of languages is one that has obviously

FIG. 62. The Nordic type.

had a good deal of polishing and planing down, and this again supports the idea of an origin in the Northern Steppes.

The people who originally spoke the language have been called Aryan, but that term should have been applied rather to the Asiatic section of this language group. Indo-Italo-Celto-Germanic has been suggested and has been shortened into Indo-Germanic. For this term the alternative of 'Indo-European' has come into use, but Dr. Giles suggests 'Wiros' for the people who spoke these tongues, since a word much like this has at one time or other been the word for 'Man' in most of these languages.

We feel that it is useful at present to think of the ancestral language of the Indo-European family as having been spoken by a people, whom we may call 'Wiros', in the steppe, somewhere between Hungary and Turkestan.

Whether the Wiros were long-heads or broad-heads or a mixture of both is more than we can say, but the Northern Steppe does seem to have been the home of long-heads in early times. It may well be that with the advance of phonetics we may have some light thrown on the probable sounds that characterized the very early languages of the group, and from that we may be able to draw some inferences as to the physical characters of the people who set the linguistic fashion. We know for example that the abundant use of *k*, *qu*, and *f* in languages suggests a people with short upper lips, but if *p* is used instead we are dealing with people who have long upper lips. We also know that long upper lips are very generally associated with the broad-heads of Central Europe and short upper lips with the long-heads of North-West Europe. The variants of the *s* sound are linked up with differences of the front part of the mouth. But this study is still quite in its infancy.

The languages of the highland zone from the Pyrenees to Armenia are a more difficult study, as it is evident that the languages of the Northern Steppe-folk have entered in. Basque does not connect itself with any of the other languages of Europe, though it has recently been said to show resemblances to some of the unclassified tongues spoken in the Caucasus.

In quite recent years Hittite tablets from Boghaz Keui near the Halys in Asia Minor have been studied, and the names of Mitra, Varuna, Indra, and the Nāsatyas have been made out from tablets of the fourteenth century B.C. These names are also known as those of deities worshipped by the Aryan conquerors of India, and their forms are distinct from those which later on were used by the Iranians of Persia. It seems on the whole that at Boghaz Keui and in India we have features derivable from a common source, and it also seems that this element in Hittite is traceable back rather to the Northern Steppe-folk by way of the Bosphorus and Thrace, than to Iran or India. It is likely that languages influenced from the Northern Steppe, probably at least as much by way of Thrace as from Iran, were spoken in ancient Asia Minor, at least in the second millennium B.C. The languages, however, seem not to have been fundamentally of the same family as those of the Wiros, and some students allege that they have a common non-Wiro foundation, to which has been given the name Asianic. It is probable that this common foundation may be near to the original tongue of the Armenoid variety of the Alpine Race.

The affinities of Elamite must be left undiscussed for the present; it is in a special degree an unsolved problem. It has recently been claimed that Sumerian shows kinship with ancient languages of Eastern Asia Minor; if so, it has sprung from the Asianic stock from which Hittite developed. It is interesting that there should be hints, as we have seen, that some of the Sumerians were broad-headed, like most of the inhabitants of Asia Minor.

APPENDIX

Some measurements of skulls from Kish, extracted from the work of L. H. Dudley Buxton in S. Langdon's *Excavations at Kish*, vol. i (1924).

	Length.	Breadth.	Cranial Index.	Maximum (or Basi-bregmatic) Height.
	mm.	mm.	%	mm.
No. 3	193	129	66·84	137
No. 4	191	132	69·43	127
No. 5	193	134	69·43	133
No. 6	173	142	82·08	—
No. 7	189	128	67·70	—
No. 8	184	135 ?	73·37 ?	— possibly female
No. 9	178	120 ?	67·42 ?	— possibly female

BOOKS

SMITH, G. ELLIOT. *The Ancient Egyptians* (London, 1911).
RIPLEY, W. Z. *The Races of Europe* (London, 1900).
FLEURE, H. J. *The Peoples of Europe* (London, 1922).
CHILDE, V. GORDON. *The Aryans* (London, 1926).
Cambridge Ancient History, vol. ii, ch. ii (Cambridge, 1924).
Cambridge History of India, vol. i (Cambridge, 1922).
GILES, P. *Manual of Comparative Philology* (London, 2nd ed., 1901).

10

Chronological Summary

WE have seen that as the northern ice cap was retreating, the zones of ocean storms and westerly winds followed it; thus the region with the heaviest rainfall moved northwards. By about 6500 B.C. it had reached a belt just north of the Alpine highlands and throughout this region dense oak forests with thick undergrowth were spreading from the south-east; the only open spaces left were places swept by salt winds, the chalk and limestone hills, some patches of sandy loess stretching intermittently just north of the Carpathians, and the great loess belt of South Russia.

At the same time the Sahara, which had hitherto been a grassy steppe rich in hoofed animals hunted by a large human population, began to grow drier; this caused many of the animals to migrate to more favoured localities, and many of the hunters followed them. The distribution of a microlithic flint industry suggests that at this time some of the human inhabitants of this region passed over the Straits of Gibraltar and across the east of Spain, and while some mixed with the indigenous populations in the north and west, others traversed the open patches of loess to South Russia and Turkestan, whither the main body of Solutrean hunters had retreated earlier.

It seems likely that other inhabitants of the Sahara passed to the south, to the grass-lands of Northern Nigeria, but of this we have at present no direct evidence. We are on surer ground when we state that others occupied the margins of the Nile Valley, especially the valley sides of the Mokattam Hills and the northern fringe of the Delta, while further evidence suggests an eastward extension to Palestine, Syria, Mesopotamia, the Vindhya Hills of India, and even Ceylon.

The first group, long-headed dark people of medium stature, must have coalesced with the more robust inhabitants of the Russian and Turkestan steppes and loess. This combination we have termed the Northern Steppe-folk, and we have suggested that they were the ancestors of those types now known as Nordic, and that they evolved a speech which was ancestral to that group of languages known as Aryan or Indo-European.

The latter group, long-headed dark people, small in the west but attaining rather taller stature in Arabia, we have called the Southern Steppe-folk; these were, we believe, the ancestors of those types now known as Mediterranean and Semitic. In North Africa they developed the ancestral form of what are now known as the Hamitic tongues still spoken by the Kabyles, Shawiya, and Tuaregs, while in Arabia their speech was Semitic, the ancestral form of the Babylonian, Phoenician, Hebrew, and Arabic tongues.

Meanwhile between the two steppe regions another type of man was apparently spreading in the mountain zone as the ice and snow diminished. These men had broad heads and dark hair and their descendants in Europe are to-day called the Alpine Race. Those in the west are somewhat short in stature and of a thick-set build, while those in the Illyrian portion of the Balkan Peninsula and in Asia Minor are tall, with projecting noses and very high heads; the latter are frequently called Armenoid. A type rather like the Western Alpine inhabits the mountains between Armenia and Tibet. The original language of the Alpines has disappeared, though it has been suggested that remnants of the Western Alpine speech may be found in the valleys of the Pyrenees, as the Basque tongue, and of the Caucasus; this is, however, very doubtful. The foundation of the languages spoken in the Hittite Empire points to a group of languages, which has been termed Asianic; this, we are suggesting, included the original tongue of the Eastern Alpines or Armenoids of Anatolia.

The first certain evidence we have of these Alpines in Europe is in a deposit in a cave at Ofnet in Bavaria and dates from Azilian times, but if it should be proved that certain graves at Solutré in which rather broad-headed skulls are found really date from the age claimed for them, we must place their arrival, or that of their related forerunners, in East France before the close of the Aurignacian period.

It would seem that it was some time between 6000 and 5000 B.C. that the first elements of a settled civilization were evolved, and we suggest that it should be sought either in the Upper Valley of the Euphrates or just where that river leaves the mountains and passes through the foot-hills before debouching on to the Mesopotamian Plain. We have suggested that the chief discoveries which led to this settled life were made by members of the Eastern Alpine or Armenoid Race as they came into contact with members of the Southern Steppe-folk just south of the mountain zone. These discoveries were the cultivation of wheat and barley, the shaping of stone implements by grinding, the making of pottery, the invention of spinning and weaving, and the discovery that the ores of metal could be melted and cast in a mould. It seems likely, too, that the erection of permanent houses dates from about the same time.

So far our reconstruction of early civilization has been a matter of inference; our earliest positive evidence comes from two centres belonging to the same period. On the site of what was later the city of Susa we find a settlement, founded, we believe, about 5000 B.C. or perhaps a little earlier. The people of this settlement had fine pottery, made in imitation of leather work; they had copper tools and woven linen, and, it is believed, they cultivated grain, though they had no domesticated animals but the dog. In addition they had finely flaked flint implements which remind us of the laurel-leaf blades of the Solutrean culture.

At Badari in Egypt there have lately been found the remains of an almost contemporary people. These used fine pottery, not so well made as that from Susa, but formed like it on a leather model. They had beads and pins of copper, ground stone axes, and flint implements like those of Susa. These people entered Egypt, we believe, from Palestine, before rather than after 5000 B.C.

Who these people were we do not know. They seem to have been long-headed, as were the people of Susa, but no detailed description of their skeletons has yet appeared. We are inclined to think that both peoples are different groups of Southern Steppe-folk, perhaps with some slight admixture of the people of the Northern Steppe, whence they may have obtained their special form of the art of flint flaking by pressure. We think that they had picked up the art of agriculture, weaving and pot-making, and perhaps some slight knowledge of the working of metal, from the folk in the north of Syria or the Upper Euphrates Valley.

The village site at Susa was abandoned suddenly. We have attributed this to a period of spring floods which we believe occurred about 4500 B.C. This we think was due to that rising of the land and consequent increase in the area of winter snow in the mountains, which in the Alpine regions of Europe is known as the Gschnitz stage. On a much higher site not far from Susa, known as Tepeh Musyan, an identical culture lasted later, and rather later still we find settlements with similar pottery at Abu Sharain and Tell el-'Obeid in the plain of Mesopotamia.

The Badarian culture seems to pass into the Early Predynastic civilization of Egypt, which we believe began about 4800 B. C. Other peoples were soon attracted to the banks of the Nile and developed their characteristic pottery. With the elevation of the land, which we have associated with the Gschnitz stage, new people entered the Delta, bringing with them the art of agriculture and domesticated animals, the rudiments of a calendar denoting a solar year, and other elements of true civilization. At the same time appeared higher up the Nile, possibly from the Arabian Desert on the east, a fresh people who were skilled in the art of making stone bowls. These learnt to make pots in imitation of these stone bowls, and developed the art of river navigation, which had probably been initiated by their predecessors.

Between 4000 and 3500 B.C. a new people arrived in Mesopotamia, almost certainly from the south. These were the Sumerians, who for long ruled in a number of city states near the head of the Persian Gulf. Whence they came is uncertain, but soon after their arrival we find them with a fully developed civilization. They grew wheat and barley, they made pottery and bricks and with the latter built temples of considerable size. They wove cloth, and kept milch kine; they were highly

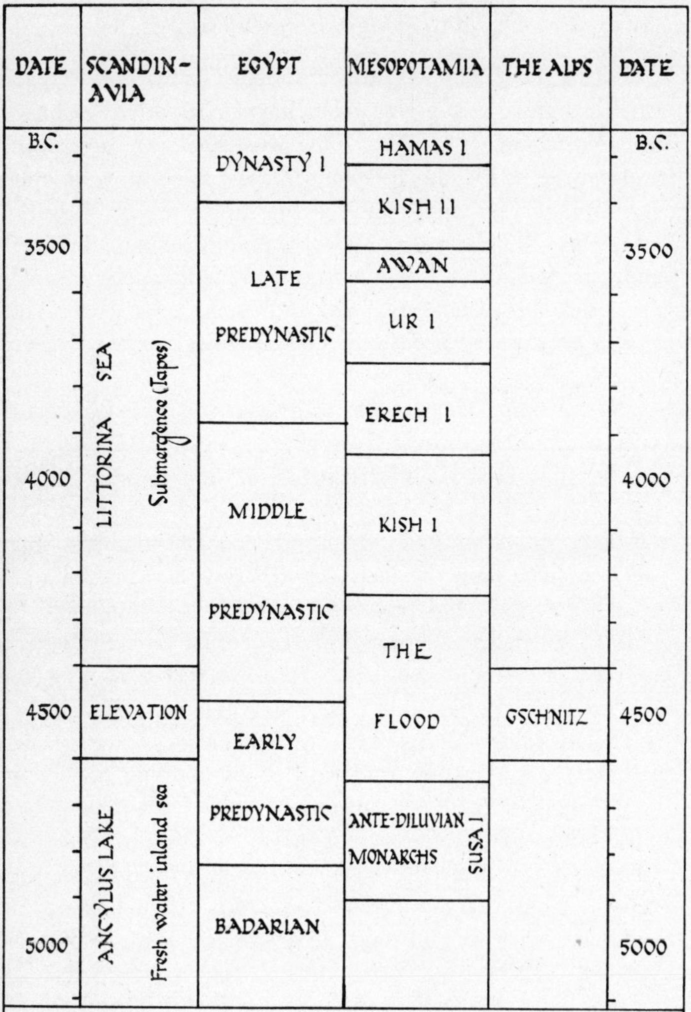

DATE	SCANDIN-AVIA	EGYPT	MESOPOTAMIA	THE ALPS	DATE
B.C.		DYNASTY 1	HAMAS 1		B.C.
			KISH II		
3500		LATE PREDYNASTIC	AWAN		3500
			UR 1		
	LITTORINA SEA — Submergence (Tapes)		ERECH 1		
4000		MIDDLE PREDYNASTIC	KISH 1		4000
4500	ELEVATION	EARLY PREDYNASTIC	THE FLOOD	GSCHNITZ	4500
	ANCYLUS LAKE — Fresh water inland sea		ANTE-DILUVIAN MONARCHS — SUSA 1		
5000		BADARIAN			5000

Fig. 63. Chart of the early ages in Egypt and Mesopotamia.

Note. The chart reads, in order of time, from the bottom upwards.

skilled in metal work, had a form of writing on clay tablets, which was long past its infancy, and evolved an elaborate system of commercial law. The first inscription of theirs that we possess must date from before 3650 B.C., and was set up by the second monarch of the first dynasty of Ur.

About the time of the arrival of the Sumerians in Mesopotamia there arrived on the eastern side of the Nile Delta some nomad tribes with sheep and goats, who settled the eastern part of that area, thus cutting off the corn-growers from contact with their relatives in Palestine and Syria. About the same time a Libyan tribe, called the Tehennu, settled on the western side, so that the agricultural group was hemmed in by two pastoral tribes. Later on another people, perhaps further invaders from the Arabian Desert, made themselves masters of Upper Egypt and conquered the Nile Valley between Cairo and the First Cataract; soon afterwards they conquered the Delta under Menes, who became king of a united Egypt about 3400 B.C.

Meanwhile in the island of Crete there had been living for many centuries a people who made very fine highly burnished pottery and used, for the most part, implements of stone and obsidian. Whether or no they cultivated grain or kept domesticated beasts is uncertain, but it seems likely that towards the close of the period they were not wholly unacquainted with copper tools, though they were probably ignorant of the processes of working in metal. A similar state of civilization was in existence in many, if not most, of the isles in the Aegean Sea, and the people of Melos were carrying on an extensive trade in implements of obsidian, a volcanic glass found in that island.

Lastly in Turkestan, a civilization had arisen at the foot of the Kopet Dagh Mountains. The people here cultivated wheat and barley, though at first they kept no domesticated animals. They possessed a few implements of copper, which they must have acquired by way of trade. The art of pot-making, which had passed its earliest stage, seems to have reached them from somewhere in Asia Minor.

Thus we find that nearly all the elements that distinguish civilized man from the savage had been discovered before 5000 B.C., and that before 3400 B.C. these had spread up the Nile, at any rate as far as the First Cataract, to the Persian Gulf, apparently through Asia Minor to the islands of the Aegean Sea and to the southern edge of the Turkestan Steppe. So far, however, we have met with none of these elements on the mainland of Europe.

INDEX

A-an-ni-pad-da, 86, 88, 90.
Aaronsohn, A., 16, 18.
Abel, 42.
Abu Rasain, 85.
Abu Sharain, 17, 21, 51, 52, 84, 86, 87, 91, 92, 142.
Abyssinia, 19.
Adab, 17, 21, 50.
Aegean Sea, 98, 99, 105, 106, 110, 144, 145.
Afghanistan, 19.
Africa, 10, 15, 19, 32, 35-7, 43, 54, 62, 72, 73, 78, 98, 121-3, 126, 139.
Alagheuz, 48.
Albright, W. F., 86.
Aleppo, 48, 96.
Alexander, 63.
Algeria, 44, 121, 133.
Allen, Grant, 15.
Alpine race, 137, 139, 140.
Alps, 8, 73, 124, 127, 128, 130, 132, 133, 138, 142, 143.
America, 22, 30, 31, 59, 120, 128.
amethyst, 77.
Anah, 16, 17.
Anatolia, 17-19, 92, 96, 99, 104-6, 109, 118, 129, 140.
Anau, 9, 10, 30, 35, 92, 94, 112-15, 118, 119, 126, 132.
Andrae, W., 85.
Antediluvian monarchs, 82, 143.
antelope, 66, 70.
Anzety, 78.
Arabia, 14, 16, 17, 32, 37, 39, 40, 62, 71, 74, 80, 81, 111, 121-4, 134, 139.
Arabic language, 135, 139.
Aral Sea, 111, 124.
Armenia, 19, 35, 48, 127, 128, 133, 136, 140.
Armenian language, 135.
Aryan people, 135, 136, 138, 139.
Ashmolean Museum, 81, 101, 103-5, 107, 109.
Asshur, 17, 85, 90.
Asia, 8-10, 32, 35-8, 54, 60, 62, 72, 80, 92, 94 98, 106, 112, 124, 128, 134.

Asia Minor, 16-19, 28, 48, 60, 61, 82, 99, 106, 111, 119, 123, 127, 128, 130-2, 136, 137, 140, 145.
Asianic languages, 137, 140.
Asinus taeniopus, 37.
Askabad, 110-12.
ass, 36, 37, 39, 40, 43, 66, 78, 80.
Assiût, 56.
Assyria, 10.
Assyrian language, 134.
Atlantic Ocean, 53, 54, 120.
Atreus (Attarissijas), 82.
Aures mountains, 44, 121.
Aurignacian period, 37, 130, 131, 140.
Australians, 12.
Awan, 143.
Azilian culture, 10.
Azilian period, 140.

Babylon, 82.
Babylonia, 10.
Babylonian language, 134, 139.
Badari, 53, 55-8, 60-2, 66, 67, 70, 71, 74, 84, 115, 124, 141-3.
Badtibira, 19.
Bagdad, 18.
Balikh, 86.
Balkan peninsula, 127, 128, 130, 140.
Balkash lake, 124.
Baltic languages, 135.
Baltic region, 12, 60, 73.
Balulu, 90.
Bami, 111.
Bandar Abbas, 95.
Barbary sheep, 35, 66, 78.
barley, 16, 19, 44, 55, 72, 74, 117, 124, 140, 142, 144.
Basque language, 133, 136, 140.
Bavaria, 126, 140.
Bedouin, 44, 81.
Belgium, 126.
Bender Bushire, 17, 51.
Berlin, 112.
Berosus, 81, 95.
Biffen, Sir Roland, 18.
Bismya, 50.
bison, 7, 30.

Index

Black Sea, 111, 124.
Boghaz Keui, 136, 137.
Bojanus, L., 32.
Bos brachyceros, 32.
Bos macroceros, 32, 33.
Bos namadicus, 32.
Bos palaeotaurus, 32.
Bos primigenius, 32, 33.
Bosphorus, 137.
Brandt, J. F., 35.
Breasted, J. H., 16, 63, 80.
British Museum, 51.
Bronze Age, 38, 130.
Brunton, G., 56, 58.
Bulgaria, 181.
Burrows, Ronald M., 110.
Buxton, L. H. Dudley, 131, 137.

Cain, 42.
Cairo, 42, 66, 144.
calendar, 72.
camel, 9, 36, 37, 118.
Canis poutiatini, 8, 10.
Cappadocia, 90.
Capsian culture, 8, 10, 30, 38, 39, 55, 62, 111, 124, 126.
carnelian, 90.
Carpathians, 30, 128, 138.
Caspian Sea, 110, 111, 124.
Casson, S., 111.
Caton-Thompson, Miss, 56.
cattle, 10, 31, 32, 38–40, 43, 72, 84, 88, 92, 110, 117.
Caucasus mountains, 111, 119, 127, 133, 136, 140.
Cautley, Sir P. T., 32.
Celtic languages, 134.
Ceylon, 8, 139.
Childe, V. Gordon, 13, 110, 138.
Constantine, 44.
copper, 47, 58, 63, 70, 71, 73, 74, 77, 79, 82, 84, 88–90, 92, 118, 141, 144.
coup-de-poing, 20.
Crete, 36, 98, 99, 105, 106, 108–10, 116, 144.
Crimea, 18.
Cyclades, 106.
Cyprus, 17, 111, 124.

Danish shell-mounds, 10, 11.
Dawkins, R. M., 106.
Delaporte, L., 96.
Denmark, 7, 11, 59, 60.
Depéret, C., 73.
desert, 16, 37, 38, 40, 43, 44, 46, 71, 74, 78, 80, 81, 110, 134, 142, 144.
Dilmun, 17, 95.
Dingo, 9, 10.
Diospolis Parva, 63.
Dnieper, 124.
dog, 8–10, 12, 39, 40, 47, 48, 62, 117, 118, 134, 141.
Dörpfeld, W., 112.
Doughty, C. M., 122.
Duerst, J. U., 32, 35, 37.
Dushak, 111.

Eanna, 93.
East Indies, 122.
Egypt, 8, 10, 15–17, 26, 28, 29, 32, 37, 43–5, 54, 56, 61, 63, 66, 71, 72, 74, 78–80, 84, 88, 90, 92, 98, 104, 106, 115, 118, 121, 123, 134, 141–4.
Egyptians, 29, 37, 54, 116, 121, 127, 138.
einkorn, 18.
Elam, 92.
Elamites, 92, 137.
emmer, 16, 18, 44, 54, 72.
Enmerkar, 94.
Erech, 17, 21, 84, 90, 93, 94, 96.
Eridu, 17, 19, 21, 51, 84.
Euphrates, 16, 17, 19, 21, 61, 82, 84, 92, 122, 140, 141.
Europe, 7, 8, 10, 12–14, 21, 30, 32, 36, 38, 46, 53, 60, 62, 98, 122, 126, 127, 132–4, 136, 138, 139, 142, 145.
European plain, 8.
Evans, Sir Arthur, 62, 98, 99, 101, 103–7, 109, 110.

Falconer, H., 32.
Fara, 90.
Fayûm, 17, 56, 58.
Fertile Crescent, 14, 16, 17, 20, 22, 26, 28, 34, 44, 46, 98, 131, 132.
First Cataract, 144, 145.
Flanders, 133.

Index

Fleure, H. J., 138.
flint, 8, 20, 47, 52, 55, 56, 58, 59, 62, 63, 70, 79, 85, 90, 116, 141.
Flood, The, 82, 84, 85, 143.
Florence, 133.
forest, 7, 8, 10, 13-15, 22, 24, 30-2, 38, 60, 138.
Frioul language, 133.
Frankfort, H., 47, 48, 50, 52, 61, 66, 67, 71, 75, 76, 80, 90, 92, 94, 96, 115, 116, 118, 119.
Furfooz, 126.
Furfooz skulls, 125.

Galicia, 30, 38.
garnet, 79.
Gautier, J. G., 50.
Genesis, Book of, 84.
Germany, 38.
Gibraltar, Straits of, 138.
Giles, P., 135, 138.
glaciation, 7, 39, 53.
glaciers, 8.
Gmelin, J. F., 35.
goat, 9, 31, 35, 40, 43, 78, 109, 118, 144.
Greece, 10, 18, 99, 110.
Greek language, 134.
Greek temple, 23.
Gschnitz stage, 8, 12, 19, 20, 51, 53, 73, 142, 143.

haematite, 77, 90.
Hall, H. R., 51, 85, 86, 88, 94, 95.
Halys, 136.
Hamasi, 143.
Hamite, 123.
Hamitic languages, 134, 139.
Harappa, 94.
Hattic people, 90.
Hawes, C. H. and H. B., 110.
Hebrew language, 134, 139.
Hermon, Mt., 16-18.
Hindu Kush, 30, 60, 124.
Hindustan, 32.
Hittites, 82, 90, 121, 127, 129, 136, 137, 140.
Höck, F., 19.

horse, 7, 30, 36, 37, 39, 47, 48, 117, 118, 124, 134.
Hungary, 30, 124, 136.

Ice Age, 122.
Illyria, 140.
India, 8, 32, 94, 95, 122, 136-9.
Indian Ocean, 111, 124.
Indo-European, 135, 136, 139.
Indra, 136.
Indus, 124.
Iran, 92, 95, 110, 137.
Iranians, 123, 136.
Isis, 72.
Italy, 106.

jackal, 10.
Java, 9.
Jebel el Arak, 75, 76.
Jemdet Nasr, 90.
Jordan, 16.
Judaea, 17, 18.
Jutland, 59.

Kabyles, 133, 139.
Kalaat Sherkat, 85.
Kara, 111.
Keneh, 74.
Kerkha, 17, 21, 46, 47.
Kerkûk, 17, 85.
Kermanshah, 17, 18.
Khazneh Tepe, 85.
King, L. W., 96.
Kish, 17, 21, 84, 90-4, 96, 130, 137, 143.
Knossos, 82, 98, 99, 103-7, 110.
Kopet Dagh, 35, 110, 111, 119, 144.
Körnicke, F., 18.
Kurdestan, 18.
kurgans, 9, 111, 112, 114, 115.

Ladak, 36.
Ladin language, 133.
Lagash, 17, 21, 90.
Lamothe, L., 73.
Lampre, G., 50.
Langdon, S., 88, 91-5, 137.
lapis lazuli, 77, 90.
Larak, 17, 19, 21.
Larsa, 17, 21.

Index

Latin language, 134.
La Tourasse, 10.
Libyan desert, 17, 37, 40, 43, 44, 78.
Libyans, 37, 67, 68, 78, 80, 144.
Liguria, 106.
lion, 89, 90.
loess, 8, 30, 124, 138, 139.
Lop Nor, 37.
Louvre, The, 49, 75.
Lydekker, R., 35.

Macalister, R. A. S., 13.
Mackay, E., 90.
Magasá, 100, 101, 106, 108.
Magdalenian period, 32, 38, 130.
malachite, 70, 90.
Malay, 94.
Malaya, 32.
mammoth, 7.
Manchuria, 128.
Marshall, Sir John, 94, 95.
Mediterranean, 7, 17, 36, 53, 73, 78, 106, 110, 124, 132.
Mediterranean race, 126, 132, 139.
Melos, 99, 106, 144.
Menes, 63, 64, 80, 90, 144.
Merv, 110, 111.
Mes-an-ni-pad-da, 86.
Meskemgašer, 93.
Mesopotamia, 16, 19, 21, 24, 32, 34, 37, 43, 53, 60, 81, 82, 88, 92, 94–6, 98, 104, 111, 116, 118, 124, 130, 139, 140, 142–4.
microlithic flints, 8, 30, 55, 62, 138.
millet, 16, 70, 79.
Mitra, 136.
Moab, 16, 17, 18.
Mohenjo-daro, 95.
Mokattam hills, 8, 17, 55, 62, 139.
Mongolia, 38.
Mongols, 39, 41.
Montelius, O., 52, 59.
Morgan, J. de, 46, 52, 53, 61.
Mugem, 10, 126.
Mugem skulls, 125.
Muscat, 95.
Myres, J. L., 14, 52, 60.

Nāsatyas, 136.
Naxos, 99, 106.

Neolithic Age, 32.
Newberry, P. E., 29, 65, 71, 72, 78, 80.
Nigeria, 139.
Nile, 10, 14–16, 17, 26, 37, 43, 44, 52, 53, 60, 62, 63, 65, 67, 69–75, 78, 80, 122–4, 132, 139, 142, 144, 145.
Nile Delta, 17, 25, 55, 62, 66, 71–6, 78, 80, 112, 134, 139, 142, 144.
Nin-Khursag, 86.
Nippur, 17, 21, 81, 82.
Nordic type, 135, 139.
Nubia, 67.

Oannes, 96, 97.
Ob, 30.
Obermaier, H., 13.
obsidian, 48, 58, 85, 90, 144.
Ofnet, 126, 140.
Ofnet skulls, 125.
Okhotsk Sea, 38.
olive, 78.
olive oil, 72.
Olivier, G. A., 16.
Ormuz, Straits of, 95.
Osiris, 72.
Ovis aries palustris, 35.
Ovis arkal, 35.
Ovis orientalis, 35.
Ovis vignei arkal, 35, 36.
ox, 7, 36, 110.
Oxford, 81, 101, 103, 104, 105, 107, 109.

Palaeolithic Age, 7, 21, 30.
Palaikastro, 99, 106.
Palestine, 8, 16, 17, 19, 59, 72, 73, 76, 139, 141, 144.
Pamirs, 128, 130, 132.
Panicum colonum, 70.
Paros, 99.
patesi, 93.
Pectunculus, 102, 106.
Percival, J., 18, 29.
Persia, 10, 16, 39, 50, 121, 123, 124, 136.
Persian Gulf, 17, 20, 21, 53, 94, 95, 111, 122, 124, 142, 145.
Persian kings, 46.
Persian language, 134.

Index

Petrie, Sir Flinders, 56, 58, 63–5, 67, 80.
Pézard, M., 51.
Phoenician language, 139.
Pianosa, 106.
Pleistocene period, 32, 53.
porphyry, 79.
pottery, 8, 11, 12, 28, 47–52, 56, 61–79, 84–7, 90–2, 98–102, 104, 106, 115–18, 140–2, 144.
Predmost, 126.
Przewalski's horse, 37, 38.
Pumpelly, R., 111, 112, 114, 115, 119.
Punjab, 35, 94, 124.
Pyrenees, 128, 133, 136, 140.

Qau, 56.

red deer, 7, 117.
Red Sea, 17, 71, 111, 134.
reindeer, 7.
Rice, B., 27.
Ripley, W. Z., 138.
Rivers, W. H. R., 132.
Roman Empire, 32.
Romansch language, 133.
Roumania, 30.
Russia, 18, 30, 31, 38, 60, 111, 138, 139.
Rütimeyer, L., 32, 35.

Sahara, 7, 14, 30, 39, 40, 59, 62, 122, 133, 134, 138, 139.
Sanskrit language, 134.
Sardinia, 106.
Scandinavia, 143.
Schliemann, H., 82.
Schmidt, Dr. H., 112, 114, 115.
Schweinfurth, G., 19.
Semite, 123, 127, 139.
Semitic languages, 92, 134.
Sequence dates, 63–78.
Sergi, G., 126.
serpentine, 77.
Shamash, 93.
Sharon, Plain of, 17, 73.
Shawiya, 44, 121, 133, 139.
sheep, 31, 34, 35, 37, 40, 78, 80, 109, 117, 118, 134, 144.

Siberia, 30.
Sicily, 106.
silver, 77.
Sinaitic peninsula, 17, 59, 70.
Sind, 95.
Sippar, 17, 19, 21.
Slavonic languages, 135.
Smith, G. Elliot, 29, 80, 121, 122, 131, 132, 138.
Smyrna, 18.
Sollas, W. J., 13.
Solutreans, 30, 31, 38, 48, 58–60, 124, 126, 139, 140, 141.
Spain, 8, 15, 138.
Spaniards, 30.
Stapf, O., 20.
steppe, 7, 16, 30–2, 35, 37–40, 42, 43, 60, 61, 81, 110, 124, 126, 127, 134, 135, 138, 139, 145.
Strauss, T., 18.
Studer, T., 8.
Sumerians, 37, 40, 51, 52, 81, 86, 90–3, 95, 96, 105, 121, 130–2, 137, 142, 144.
Šuruppak, 17, 19, 20, 21, 84, 90.
Susa, 21, 24, 29, 46, 48–53, 59, 61, 72, 76, 82, 84, 86, 90–2, 94, 99, 115, 118, 124, 132, 141–3.
Sweden, 7, 59.
Switzerland, 32, 35, 127.
Syria, 17, 18, 48, 61, 71–6, 78, 79, 92, 96, 139, 141, 144.

Tagus, 126.
Tardenoisian culture, 8, 62.
Tarim basin, 38.
Tatlu, 111.
Tehennu, 78, 144.
Tell-el-Judaidah, 85.
Tell-el-Lahm, 85.
Tell el-'Obeid, 35, 51, 52, 60, 85, 86, 88, 89, 91, 92, 96, 142.
Tell es-Semen, 86.
Tell Zeidân, 86.
Tepeh Musyan, 21, 50–3, 61, 86, 91, 142.
Teutonic languages, 134.
Thebes, 74, 134.

Thompson, R. Campbell, 51, 84.
Thrace, 137.
Tibet, 36, 140.
Tierra del Fuego, 12.
Tiflis, 111.
Tigris, 17, 19, 21, 61, 82, 122.
Tocharian language, 134.
Transcaucasia, 18.
Tripoli, 19.
Troy, 112.
Troy, tale of, 82.
Tuaregs, 133, 139.
tundra, 7, 30, 38.
Turkestan, 9, 30, 32, 35, 38, 60, 110, 111, 119, 124, 134, 136, 139, 144, 145.
Turko-Tatars, 9.
turquoise, 48, 77.

Ur, 17, 34, 40, 51, 52, 84–6, 88, 90, 96, 105, 143, 144.
Ural mountains, 124.
Ur-Nina, 131.
Urumiya, 50.
urus, 32.

Varuna, 136.
Vavilov, N. I., 19.
Vindhya hills, 139.
Volga, 60.
Vosges, 38.

Wadi Hammamat, 71, 74.
Wadi Samara, 70.
Weld-Blundell, C. J., 81.
Weld-Blundell prism, 81, 83, 93.
wheat, 16, 18, 22, 29, 44, 82, 117, 124, 140, 142, 144.
Wiros, 135, 136, 137.
wolf, 10, 117.
Woolley, C. L., 51, 86, 88.

Xisuthros, 84.

yak, 36.
Yugo-Slavia, 18, 27.

Zagros mountains, 16–19, 21, 46, 94.
Ziûsuddu, 84.

Printed in England at the OXFORD UNIVERSITY PRESS
By John Johnson Printer to the University